Creative Problem Solving

In the Classroom

**The Educator's Handbook
for Teaching Effective
Problem Solving Skills**

Joel E. McIntosh, M.S.Ed.
April W. Meacham, M.S.Ed.

Prufrock
Press Post Office Box 8813
Waco, Texas 76714-8813
1-800-998-2208

Acknowledgments

We would like to thank Dr. Susan Johnsen, Baylor University, whose mentorship, expertise, and encouragement (prodding) were instrumental in the writing of this book and in so much else we have done since meeting her.

We would like to thank Dr. Osborn, Dr. Parnes, Dr. Torrance, and Dr. Treffinger. Their pioneering work has made creative thinking available to the many. Without their work, this book would not have been possible. In fact, this book can claim to be little more than an explanation and application of the principles developed and articulated by these leaders in the field of education.

Finally, any acknowledgments for this book must include the thousands of readers and supporters of *The Prufrock Journal, The Journal of Secondary Gifted Education*. Time after time, this group has been a source of support, encouragement, and good will.

Table of Contents

Preface

This book is divided into five sections. The Introduction offers an overview of the importance and need for creative thinking and creative problem solving. Chapter One offers an in-depth look at the thinking skills in which students need to develop a proficiency before attempting the creative problem solving process. Those students who have training in the basic thinking skills required for creative problem solving will be more successful when called upon to generate the good ideas required for a productive problem solving session (Osborn, 1957).

Chapter One also provides a number of ready-to-use activities for both the elementary and secondary classroom. These activities are of two types. The first type is not specifically tied to any classroom content. For example, in one such activity, students generate ways to improve their lunch period at school. The purpose of these activities is to provide the teacher with a ready-made activity for teaching the specific thinking skill identified regardless of the discipline involved. These activities are offered as "starter activities" for students new to the various strategies involved.

The second type of activity offers an example of the thinking strategies discussed as they might be applied to traditional content within a discipline of study. For example, in one activity, students consider possible topics for a research paper on the American Civil War—an activity specific to the history classroom. Given the limitations of space and the many disciplines, only one discipline-specific activity is provided for each strategy. While activities of this latter type are ready-to-use only for teachers of the discipline involved, any teacher may create a content oriented activity using these activities as a model.

Chapter Two provides an in-depth look at the creative problem solving process. Each step is explored in detail, and suggestions for first-timers to the process are included. Chapters Three and Four offer a number of classroom activities that guide students through the creative problem solving process. Chapter Three contains activities for the elementary classroom, and Chapter Four provides activities for the secondary classroom.

Read this book cover-to-cover or pick and choose among the strategies presented. Either method will be effective in helping you lead students to a better understanding of productive thinking and the creative problem solving process. But, most of all, enjoy the excitement that the ideas included in this text provide students.

Introduction
The Need for Creative Problem Solving

Creativity is at the heart of innovation. It acts as the essential tool of the entrepreneur, the scientist, the artist, and anyone in a field where original insight is valued. Whether change is produced as a result of Salk's Polio vaccine, Edison's light bulb, or Job's Macintosh computer, the catalyst for forward movement in society is the creative, inventive mind.

In his book, *Applied Imagination* (1957), Alex Osborn describes the importance of creativity:

> The history of civilization is essentially the record of man's creative ability. Imagination is the cornerstone of human endeavor; it is, without doubt, responsible for man's survival as an animal; and it has caused him, as a human being, to conquer the world. It may well lead him to subdue the universe. Modern society, with its emphasis upon the progressive synthesis of technological and pure science, is admittedly dependent upon imagination as its life-blood. It is axiomatic that to think intelligently is to think creatively.

Given the importance of creativity, it is exciting to know that research clearly demonstrates that schools can significantly increase the creative behavior of students (Torrance, 1979). Those behaviors characteristic of creative individuals are available to all. The "good" idea need not be the property of a few.

Yet, in a world where creativity is so important and teachable, it is ironic that schools seldom teach the skills necessary for developing and using creativity. Students may leave our schools with study skills designed to enhance their abilities to memorize information or analytical skills to enhance their abilities to explicate a poem, but they may never be exposed to a formal thinking process that is designed to produce innovative ideas, products, and solutions.

To complicate matters, schools may be responsible for the suppression of creativity among students, especially certain groups such as girls (Dacey & Ripple, 1967; Torrance, 1963). The environment of many schools is an authoritarian one that does not value creative thinking or creative ideas (Dacey, 1989). In such an environment, creativity may falter. The need in the schools, then, is for not only a valuing of creative thinking but for the strategies that will allow educators to give students the creative thinking tools they will need to meet the challenges of an increasingly complex world.

The creative problem solving process is one strategy designed to help meet this need. The designers of the process have incorporated research on productive thinking that began in 1936 with the work of Alex Osborn (1957) and continues today. The bedrock of this research is the theory that creativity is the result of a process. Paul Torrance (1962), a leader in the study of creativity, explains that the process involves "becoming sensitive to problems, deficiencies, gaps in knowledge, missing elements, disharmonies, and so on; identifying the difficulty; searching for solutions, making guesses or formulating hypotheses about deficiencies; testing and retesting these hypotheses and possibly modifying and retesting them; and finally communicating the results."

Consider this process at work among educators. The authors of this text recently made a presentation to a group of teachers on the topic of creative teaching strategies that motivate the gifted. The teachers in the audience attended the presentation because they were sensitive to a problem in their classrooms (boredom among some gifted learners), and they had identified the difficulty (a lack of motivational teaching strategies). They were searching for a solution by attending the workshop. Afterward, they made educated guesses about which strategies would work with their gifted youngsters. Upon returning to the classroom, they tested their guesses by using those strategies—building on the ones that worked and omitting the ones that did not. Finally, when they had implemented those new strategies successfully, the teachers shared what they learned with others (most likely in the teachers' work room or over lunch in the school cafeteria).

Creative problem solving as it is outlined by Treffinger and Isaksen (1985) is a formal approach for teaching the creative process Torrance describes above. The process allows educators to teach students to think creatively and productively both in and out of the classroom. The creative problem solving process is also valuable because it empowers students to take charge of the future. This pro-active role is especially important for students living in the 1990s—a time of great change. Barbra Caroll (1990), a teacher involved with the Future Problem Solving Program (a national competition focusing on the problem solving process), explains, "Students, while having optimistic outlooks on their personal futures, often have negative attitudes toward our collective global futures. Many of these 'negative extrapolists' project present trends toward a doomsday society. Turning these pessimistic potential leaders into active agents of change, who demonstrate control of their lives and set realistic goals, is the heart of education for the future." It is also the heart of the creative problem solving process—a process that allows students to see the difficulties and problems of the present and future not as barriers to success, but as challenges to be met.

Teachers who have incorporated the creative problem solving process into their classrooms often comment that the process is liberating. It teaches students a way to break from the structures and limitations of the past and helps them become active shapers of their own lives.

As with many good educational strategies, the creative problem solving process is student centered. Using the process is quite engaging for students because they control it. They act as directors of their own research, thinking, and productivity. Teachers of such students act not as directors or teachers, but as facilitators—moving about the classroom helping students effectively use the process.

Creative problem solving also allows students to develop important small group skills. While it is often used by individuals working alone, it is especially effective when used in small groups. Because our students will be entering a world where, increasingly, decisions are made in small groups, it is important that they know and can share this process with others.

Regardless of the benefits offered by creative problem solving, teachers should remember that the process is not an educational end in itself. It is a tool for solving real-world problems. While the activities and simulations included in this book are useful for teaching the creative problem solving process, they are only a means to an end. Students must be given the opportunity to apply the process to the real problems they face in their own lives (Treffinger 1980).

Chapter 1
Divergent and Convergent Thinking

The Balance of Thought

Two types of thought—divergent and convergent thinking—are essential for effective problem solving. Divergent thinking, the type of thinking used to create ideas, and convergent thinking, the type of thinking used to judge ideas, are used in every step of the creative problem solving process. The goal of divergent thought is to generate as many ideas and opinions as possible. The goal of convergent thought is just the opposite—to use the tools of evaluation and judgment to identify only the strongest or most useful ideas. These two types of thinking work most productively when they are not intermixed (Osborn, 1963). Students should not try to judge ideas while creating them, and they should not try to create ideas while judging them. This relationship is essential for successful creative problem solving.

Consider this relationship in terms of a mountain—a mountain of ideas (see Figure One). The height of the mountain represents the number of ideas with which the learner is working. At Figure One's far left, the foot of the mountain, the learner begins with few ideas. Using the techniques of divergent thinking, the learner generates many new ideas. By the time she reaches the summit of the mountain, a great many ideas have been generated. The learner then uses the tools of convergent thinking to narrow the number of ideas down to a few or one truly strong idea.

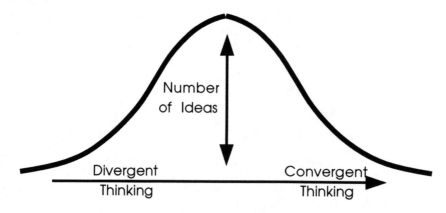

Figure One

Consider how this process might be used in an elementary class-room. During a math unit on measurement, an elementary teacher might ask students to discuss all the different items in the classroom that could be used as instruments of measurement. Students would use divergent thinking strategies to come up with a variety of responses that would be recorded by the teacher. Some examples might include paper clips, pencils, or shoes as alternatives to standard measuring devices such as rulers. The teacher would then ask the students to use convergent thinking to choose the three best items to measure surface areas such as desktops and bookshelves in the classroom.

In another elementary class, students might suggest character qualities from a variety of categories including physical appearance or personality traits. This activity could be used following almost any reading assignment. For example, after reading *Charlotte's Web*, a language arts teacher might encourage divergent thinking by asking students to brainstorm as many qualities as possible of a particular character from the story such as Wilbur. After listing as many characteristics as they can think of, students might then be asked to think convergently by choosing three qualities they have in common with the given character.

In the secondary classroom, a history teacher might ask the divergent question, "What are some of the characteristics of twentieth century American political leaders?" Using divergent thinking strategies, students in this class would generate various answers, and the teacher would record student responses. After the students generate many ideas (they reach the idea mountaintop), the teacher would ask them to use convergent thinking skills to identify the three characteristics recorded which are most likely to enable a leader to generate mass public support for his or her political agenda.

In another secondary classroom, a life science teacher might note to students that there is a strong, positive correlation between the body size and the age of animals. There is, however, a strong, negative correlation between animal body size and litter size. The teacher might ask the students to use divergent thinking to speculate as to the causes of these correlations. After recording student responses, the teacher then would ask students to use convergent thinking strategies to identify the reasons which could be tested under controlled conditions in a laboratory.

Note that in the above examples, the divergent and convergent processes do not intermix. First, students think divergently, and then, they converge on a set of ideas.

Each step of the creative problem solving process makes extensive use of divergent and convergent thinking—students first divergently think, and then, convergently think. The activities at each step in the process may be slightly different, but their purpose is to ensure that these two thinking skills work as separate but cooperative dynamics in the creative problem solving process.

Ground Rules for Divergent Thought

Divergent thinking is the ideas-generating strategy of the divergent/convergent pair. It is through divergent thought that many ideas are created. E. Paul Torrance (1979) outlines behaviors characteristic of divergent thinking. These include:

- **Fluency**—Divergent thinking produces many ideas.
- **Flexibility**—Divergent thinking produces ideas from many different categories.
- **Originality**—Divergent thinking produces ideas that are unique and innovative.
- **Elaboration**—Divergent thinking produces complex ideas that are rich in detail.

For example, ask a group of adults in what ways they might spend a fun Saturday night. At first, the group might list a number of their favorite restaurants (many ideas from the same category—fluency). Then someone might mention that she would like to attend a circus scheduled to be in town (a new category of idea—flexibility). Another mentions that he has always wanted to be a clown and that participating as a clown in the circus would be fun for him (a unique idea—original). Finally, someone in the group describes a romantic dinner on his boat at the local lake. He explains that there is a quiet cove where he would like to take his wife, cook a juicy steak dinner, and watch from the boat's deck as the burning orange sun sets (rich in detail—elaborate).

While the specific activities encouraging divergent thought are slightly different for each stage of creative problem solving, Sidney Parnes (Parnes, Noller, and Biondi, 1977), offers some very important ground rules for this type of thinking. All activities discussed later in this book are based upon the six ground rules below. Students should keep these in mind as they progress through the process.

- **Defer Judgment**—Keep your mind open to any idea generated. Never limit your options by criticizing an idea at this stage. Do not affirm an idea either. Your only purpose at this stage is to generate ideas. This is the most important of the divergent ground rules.
- **Look for Many Ideas**—The goal of the divergent phase of each step is to generate as many ideas as possible. The belief here is that "quantity breeds quality." The individual with many paths from which to choose is better off than the individual with three or four.

- **Accept All Ideas**—Never reject an idea because it seems wild or crazy. Remember that an "up-start" idea may become a "jump-start" idea, and seemingly silly ideas may inspire truly astounding ones.
- **Make Yourself "Stretch"**—Push yourself beyond normal limits. Overcome the desire to say, "Well, that's just about all I can come up with." The most original and innovative ideas are often generated very late in the divergent phase (Osborn, 1957).
- **Take Time to Let Ideas "Simmer"**—Putting an issue aside for a time and considering other matters can lead to the generation of new ideas. When you tell someone you will "sleep on it," you are intuitively recognizing the value of this ground rule. When possible, allow a period of time before you start the convergent phase of a step.
- **Seek Combinations and Be a "Hitch-Hiker"**—To generate new and original ideas, it is a good idea to combine other ideas (i.e., combinations) or build new ideas off old (i.e., hitch-hiking).

The following section offers a number of strategies or "tools" for thinking divergently. Following each strategy's explanation are several activities that ask students to apply the strategy discussed to a given problem. Both specific examples of the use of the strategies as they might be applied to traditional content and activities which are somewhat non-disciplinary in nature are provided. These activities are appropriate for use with students new to the strategies. Once familiarity is established.

Students will use all of these strategies later during the creative problem solving process. Students learning these tools for thinking before participating in the creative problem solving process will find they have a toolbox full of ways to approach each step of the process.

Divergent Activities

Divergent Warm-Up

Think for a moment about the various activities you would see were you to attend a track meet. Of course, you would see many athletes running, jumping, and participating in other competitive activities. However, you would also see many athletes doing something that, on the surface, seems to have little to do with the job of competing. You would see them warming-up for their event. They would stretch, mentally prepare, and lightly exercise. While these activities look almost entirely unrelated to the competitions at hand, they are very important.

Like the athlete, creative thinkers also need time to warm up (Torrance, 1979). One effective type of warm-up exercise, appropriately called "divergent warm-up," is suggested by Treffinger (1980). The purpose of this type of activity is to get students to think beyond rules and limitations—to get them to focus on the possible and the original.

In this type of activity, the teacher presents students with an open-ended, evocative question. The emphasis, for students, is on imagining answers that are fun, whimsical, or original. In the activity below, students examine a picture and generate some ideas about what is happening in the picture. Of course, any interesting or evocative visual could be used.

Also, rather than presenting students with a picture, the teacher could simply ask an open-ended question. For example:

- "What are some ways you could travel on a planet with no gravity?"
- "What are some ways we might improve the textbook we use for this class?"
- "If a chemical plant let off a strange gas into the atmosphere that turned the incoming light purple, how would your life be changed?"

Don Treffinger (1980) offers a number of ideas for creating questions appropriate for divergent warm-up. Treffinger suggests that students create ways to improve a product, offer endings or completions to unfinished stories or pictures, offer new uses for common objects, generate optional endings or titles for a story, or offer alternative explanations for the events depicted in a picture. The activity below is an example of this latter type of divergent warm-up.

Divergent Warm-Up Activity

Think About It

Look at the picture below for a moment.

What is happening in the picture?

What else might be happening?

What happened just before the scene in this picture?

What do you think will happen next?

Brainstorming

Brainstorming involves applying the guidelines for divergent thinking to an open-ended discussion or question. A discussion or question is open-ended when it invites many different responses and kinds of responses. For example, the question, "What are some ways to make your study time at home more efficient?" allows for many possible answers. The individual asking the question is not looking for a single, "right" response. On the other hand, a closed-ended question is designed to elicit a best or "right" answer. "On what date did Patrick Henry deliver his 'Give Me Liberty or Give Me Death' speech?" is clearly a closed-ended question.

The above is not to suggest that closed-ended questions have no place in the classroom. Rather, that brainstorming is an appropriate thinking tool for addressing open-ended questions, and is not an appropriate thinking tool for addressing closed-ended questions.

Osborn (1957) suggests that, when time allows, a brainstorming session include three phases. In the first, students brainstorm individually, writing their ideas on a piece of paper. Second, students join in a group and brainstorm ideas, writing ideas on butcher paper posted so all can see and review the group's ideas. Finally, a brainstorming session concludes with students brainstorming individually once again. Also, Osborn explains that the best ideas produced during brainstorming are often produced during the latter half of a brainstorming session. The message here is that a brainstorming session should not be concluded prematurely—students should stretch themselves.

During a traditional brainstorming session, a problem or open-ended question is posed. Often, but not necessarily, the posed problem or question begins with one of the following stems:

- In what ways might ...
- How might ...
- In what ways do ...
- How do ...

For example in an elementary social studies class, students might be studying the difference between economic needs and wants. To encourage divergent thought, the teacher might pose such a question as, "In what ways do people around the world provide shelter for themselves?" Students would respond by brainstorming all the different types of homes in which people live.

On the secondary level, the content is different but the brainstorming technique is the same. While discussing the community's decision to force Hester to wear a red letter "A" as a symbol of her adultery and as a tool for discouraging such behavior by others in the novel *The Scarlet Letter*, a high school English teacher might ask her class, "In what ways do we try to control the behaviors of others in our present culture?" or "What are some present-day 'badges of shame' we use to affect the behaviors of others?"

The following are all open-ended questions. Notice that open-ended questions and brainstorming have many applications both in and out of the classroom.

Elementary
- Language Arts—In what ways might the lives of Peter from *Superfudge* and Ramona from *Ramona the Pest* be alike? In what ways might they be different?
- Social Studies—Based upon a study of goods and services, what are some services that people your age might provide for others to earn money?
- Math—How many word problems might you come up with which include twelve pieces of candy and three children?
- Science—How many different experiments might you create which would involve the sun as a source of energy?

Secondary
- English—In what ways might adolescent life in a Puritan village and adolescent life in a Rationalist town differ?
- Social Studies—What are some social activities of families today? [Later the teacher might ask students to find parallel activities among families of the Victorian age.]
- Math—How many ways might I state the relationships in the following sentence using mathematical equations? "Rick and Jane joined their buddies at the rock concert."
- Science—If we walk into an open field, what are some of the items, animals, insects, and plants we might find? [Later this generated list would become a focus for a study of niches within an ecosystem.]

Brainstorming Activity (Elementary)

The New Kid in Town

You live in a small town with only one elementary school. Almost all the children in the school know each other. You and your classmates have all been in the same class together since kindergarten, and you all get along very well.

Jill and her family just moved to your town from a large city several hundred miles away. Jill has been in your class for one week, and you and your friends have noticed that she doesn't seem very happy. She appears to be quite shy. So far, she has only spoken in class when called upon by the teacher. She eats alone at lunch and sits by herself on the playground at recess and watches the other children play.

You and your friends would like to help Jill, but you are unsure about how to do so. You all know each other well and are very comfortable with each other. You have never had a new student in your class before.

In what ways might your class help Jill to be happier in her new school? First, brainstorm all the adjustments Jill must make. Then, brainstorm things that you can do to help Jill make these adjustments. Remember, don't make judgements (good or bad) about the ideas members of your group come up with during brainstorming.

_____

_____

_____

_____

_____

_____

_____

_____

_____

_____

_____

_____

Brainstorming Activity (Secondary)

A Whale of a Tale

Brainstorming is a way of producing many ideas. Remember that during a brainstorming session, you and your group should follow the guidelines listed below:

- **Defer judgment**—don't criticize or compliment the ideas generated by yourself or others.
- **Accept even off-the-wall ideas**—accept all ideas, even those that sound wild or crazy at first.
- **Create plenty of ideas**—"quantity breeds quality" is the principle behind this guideline.
- **Combine ideas or build one idea off another**—try creating new ideas by combining ideas or "hitch-hiking" ideas off one another.

For six years, your class has earned and saved money through candy sales, sales of magazine subscriptions, and book fairs. Finally, you earn enough money for your entire class to travel on a one week vacation together. After much thought, your class chooses to go on a week long cruise aboard a luxury liner.

Three days into the trip, on a rough and stormy evening while you and many of your classmates are playing above ship, a large wave rolls over the boat. The wave sweeps you and your friends into the sea. Swimming desperately for what seems like hours, you finally wash ashore on a small island. Upon reaching land, you collapse from exhaustion.

In the morning, one of your friends awakens you. It seems that everyone else reached the island too. After determining that everyone is in good shape, you and your friends explore the small island. On the island, you find no fresh water. You do find a few palm trees, some brush, a small number of large rocks, and two large, dirty white plastic sheets (trash that apparently washed ashore). Other than the clothes you and your friends are wearing and a lighter and some soggy cigarettes one student possesses, you find little else.

As you know that the Coast Guard must be searching for your group by now, in what ways might you and your friends use the resources you have available to aid searchers in finding you?

List your ideas below:

_____
_____
_____
_____
_____
_____
_____
_____
_____
_____
_____
_____
_____
_____
_____
_____
_____
_____
_____
                                    _____
                                    _____
                                    _____
                                    _____
                                    _____
                                    _____
                                    _____

Brainstorming Activity (Secondary—Math)

It's My Party

Mathematical relationships are all around us. The ability to see these relationships from different perspectives is the first step in the process mathematicians use to solve complex problems. Consider the information in the paragraph below.

Last Saturday night, Stan attended a party. At the party were 49 of his friends. Half of those at the party were boys and half girls. Of the girls, 20 wore earrings, and of the boys, 3 wore earrings. There were 8 couples at the party. Everyone else came single to the party.

List below as many relationships as you see in the above paragraph. Consider relationships that are equivalent, proportionate, greater than, less than, etc. Express relationships in fractions, drawings, phrases, or equations. For example, half of the party-goers are girls and half are boys. Just a few ways to express this relationship include "25 + 25 = 50," "25 + x = 50," "x = y = 25," or "There is a one to one ratio of boys to girls."

_____

_____

_____

_____

_____

_____

_____

_____

_____

_____

_____

_____

_____

_____

Attribute Listing

Attribute listing is a structured form of brainstorming developed by Crawford and refined by Osborn (Osborn, 1957). Rather than generate ideas about an entire topic, as in brainstorming, in attribute listing, students generate ideas about various aspects of a topic. For example, if an inventor wanted to design an improved chair, she might use attribute listing to do so. She would first identify the various attributes of a chair—the back, the seat, the legs. Then, she would generate ideas for improving each attribute separately. The back of the chair might have padding, be contoured, lean back, or swivel. The seat might be filled with water like a water-bed, enlarged, swivel, be contoured, or be supported with springs. The legs might lengthen or shorten, fold for easy storage, or contain springs that act as shock absorbers.

On the elementary level, attribute listing can be applied to all subject areas. In a language arts lesson on forms of letter writing, students might be asked to list the attributes of a thank you note. These generally include the date, the heading, the body, and the closing. Students might then brainstorm possible options for each of the attributes and finish the lesson by writing sample thank you notes. One such sample might be dated December 26, addressed to Aunt Sarah, and might describe the new sweater the student received from Aunt Sarah for Christmas.

An elementary science teacher might review a unit on food groups by having students identify the attributes of a balanced meal. Students could then create menus for their favorite (balanced) meals by suggesting options for each attribute.

On the secondary level, attribute listing can be used in a variety of ways. In the English classroom during a lesson on writing for an audience, a teacher might ask students to identify the various attributes of a persuasive essay on the topic of animal rights written for an adolescent audience. Such attributes might include issues involved, modes of persuasion, style of writing, and use of examples to illustrate points. Students would then generate ideas that would appeal to an adolescent audience for each of these attributes.

After a study of a national or state problem, a history or government class might be asked to identify the various attributes of the problem. The class could then generate various ideas for addressing each attribute of the problem or issue. Or, as an introduction to the problem, students might generate the questions they have about each attribute of the problem. The questions could then guide the teacher as she organizes her unit of study about the problem.

Attribute Listing (Elementary)

A Holiday Celebration

This year for the first time, your teacher and principal have agreed to allow your class to plan your own class holiday party. You must work together to plan a party that everyone will enjoy. There are many details to consider when planning a party, so your class has decided to use attribute listing to have the best party ever!

1. Next to the letters below, write some of the attributes involved in a class party. For example, the location where you choose to have the party would be one attribute, so you might list "location" next to the letter "A" below.
2. After listing attributes next to the letters below, consider all the options related to each attribute. For example, in the case of "location," brainstorm all the possible locations for a class holiday party. Don't forget to use divergent thinking.

A. _____
- _____
- _____
- _____

B. _____
- _____
- _____
- _____

C. _____
- _____
- _____
- _____

D. _____
- _____
- _____
- _____

Attribute Listing Activity (Secondary)

The All-New and Improved Study Session

George could use some help. Time after time, he finds himself staying up all night to study for his tests. George feels that staying up all night makes him less sharp when he gets to class and takes his test. He has decided to improve the ways he studies, and he has asked your group for some ideas. To offer George some ideas, you will use attribute listing to answer the questions below.

1. Next to the letters below, write some of the attributes involved in a study program. For example, the time during which you choose to study is certainly an attribute of any study program, so you might list "time" next to the letter "A" below.

2. After listing attributes next to the letters below, write down at least three ways to improve on each attribute. For instance, in the case of "time," offer ways George might improve his use of time. List your ideas below each attribute.

A. _____

-
-
-

B. _____

-
-
-

C. _____

-
-
-

D. _____

-
-
-

Attribute Listing Activity (Secondary—Social Studies)

Energy Policy

The United States is dependent on foreign nations for a large percentage of its oil and gas. Since the early 1980s, the nation's dependence has grown each year. This increasing reliance on the resources of other countries places the United States in a vulnerable position. In the activity below, your group is asked to develop some ideas for reducing this country's dependence on foreign energy.

1. Next to the letters below, write some of the attributes of this country's dependence on foreign oil. For example, the sources of energy are certainly an attribute of this issue. You might list "Sources of Energy" in the blank next to the letter "A" below.
2. After listing attributes next to the letters below, write down at least three ways to improve on each attribute. For instance, in the case of "Sources of Energy" you might list "increase exploration of domestic petroleum sources" or "offer cash incentives for domestic petroleum exploration" as ways to improve on this attribute.

A. _____

•

•

•

B. _____

•

•

•

C. _____

•

•

•

D. _____

•

•

•

Idea Checklists

Alex Osborn (1957) proposes the idea checklist as an excellent tool for helping students generate new ideas. Essentially, an idea checklist is a list of items which students use to "spur" them on to new insight. For example, if a class were discussing the many ways their classroom might be made more attractive, the students might be presented an idea checklist on which the word "glass" appears. One student might see this word and think of other containers. While thinking of other containers, she might think of a pot—a pot in which flowers grow. The student then suggests that the room be brightened up with fresh, potted flowers.

Idea checklists are easy to create. The checklists in the first two activities below were created by randomly opening the yellow pages of a phone book and looking at the headings.

In the second two activities, students work with an idea checklist proposed by Osborn (1957) and adapted by Eberle (1989) called SCAMPER. The SCAMPER checklist offers a structured way to manipulate the way students view a question, issue, or object. Manipulating one's view often generates new and original insight. SCAMPER is an acronym for the following:

- **Substitute**—A new idea or item is substituted for an idea or item proposed earlier in the idea generating session. For example, if students are examining ways a classroom might be made more attractive, a student might suggest brightening the room with fresh, potted flowers. The teacher might ask a substitution question by saying, "What are some other things [substitute] we might put in a pot which would brighten the room?" A student might answer, "We could grow herbs which would make the room smell better."
- **Combine**—Students combine two or more ideas generated earlier to create an altogether new idea. For example, the students considering ways to improve the classroom might be asked if there is a way to combine their fresh, potted flower idea and an earlier idea that brighter colors could be used on the bulletin boards. One student might suggest that a bulletin board of many flowers be created—each student could bring in a favorite flower to be pressed, labeled, and pinned to one of the bulletin boards in the classroom.
- **Adapt**—An idea generated earlier is adapted or adjusted. For instance, one student might suggest that the bulletin board of many flowers mentioned above, could be made even more interesting if the space between the board's base and the floor were decorated [adapted] with construction paper so that it looked like a pot. Then the class could draw stems from each of the flowers to the pot. The result would be a board that looked like a huge flower pot.

- **Modify, Magnify, and Minify**—Ideas are changed so that they become modified, magnified, or minified. For example, in the case of magnifying an idea, a class discussing ways to improve a classroom might be asked, "What are some ways we could make the room look larger [magnify]?" One student might suggest that the rows of desks be replaced with large circular tables. These circular tables would allow for more open space that would make the room seem larger.

- **Put to other uses**—Students examine items or ideas to see if they could serve other purposes. For instance, one student might look at a section of unused bookcase space and suggest that it be used as a display case for exceptional student products.

- **Eliminate**—Students eliminate items or objects and suggest alternatives to fill the gap. For example, in the classroom improvement session, the teacher might suggest that all the desks in the room be eliminated. The teacher would then ask students to suggest ideas for filling the gap left by the removed desks. One student might suggest throw pillows or bean-bag chairs, another might suggest two long tables for writing, and another student might suggest the installation of two computer centers.

- **Reverse or Rearrange**—Students reverse a sequence within an idea or change a pattern within the idea. In our classroom improvement example, students might suggest that the rows of desks be broken down [rearranged] into many circular groups of desks or that all the desks be rearranged in a large circle.

Whether you choose to use SCAMPER or simply a random list of items, the idea checklist has plenty of possible applications to classroom content. On the elementary level, the idea checklist can be used in social studies to help students choose possible occupations to research (using a checklist to identify categories under which more specific occupations might occur), in science to help students generate a group of items which can be used in an experiment to test magnetic attractiveness (using a checklist to identify items which might not be commonly found in the classroom), or in language arts to help students write a new ending to a story (using a checklist to develop possible situations which might occur in the new ending).

On the secondary level, the idea checklist can be used to help students develop a creative short story (using a checklist to generate characters, plots, settings, and conflicts for a story), help design an independent study unit about London in the 1600s (using a checklist to generate questions about the city during that period), or generate a list of alternative energy sources (first using a checklist to identify various forms of energy found about us).

Idea Checklist Activity (Elementary)

A Class Fund-Raiser

Your class has decided that you would like to adopt an animal from the zoo. All the animals that you are interested in adopting are quite expensive. To make this project truly a class effort, your class has decided to come up with a fund-raiser to acquire the money necessary for adoption. The more money you raise, the more exotic the animal you adopt can be.

Many other classes and groups within your school have already had fund-raisers. Your class wants to have a truly unique project to raise the most money possible. Therefore, you have decided to use an idea checklist to help you come up with original ideas. For example, in the list below, the word "Mail" appears. "Mail" might make you think of stationery. You have several classmates who are good artists, so one possibility for a fund-raiser might be to sell stationery designed by your class. You would then list the word "stationery" below next to the word "Mail."

Concrete:

Mail:

House:

Car:

Swimming Pool:

Kite:

Museum:

Idea Checklist Activity (Secondary)

Summer Vacation

Over the last six years, your classmates and you have raised money through sales of candy, sales of magazine subscriptions, and book fairs. It is now time to spend all of that money, and your class has decided to spend it on a class retreat—a week-long vacation together.

The student council has asked for lists of possible vacation ideas. To help create a list of unique ideas, the council has provided an idea checklist—a list of items that can help you generate new ideas. For example, in the list below, the word "Guitars" appears. This word might make you think of singers with guitars like George Strait, and you know that many of your friends like to listen to country-and-western singers like Strait. To see such singers in concert, you might suggest that your class travel to the Grand Old Opry in Nashville, Tennessee. You would list "Grand Old Opry & Nashville, Tennessee" below next to the word "Guitars."

Idea checklists are easy to create. The one below was created by randomly opening the yellow pages of a phone book and looking at the headings.

Boats:

Farms:

Glass:

Guitars:

Pests:

Pizza:

Veterinarians:

Idea Checklist Activity (Secondary—English)

Huckleberry Finn Again

Huckleberry Finn is the embodiment of a character type in the American culture—a mixture of both innocence and experience. The activity below will act as a pre-writing step in the writing process. It will help you develop a story line for a short story you will write in which Huck Finn finds himself in an unusual situation. Consider the many different ways Huck might react to the various settings listed below.

For each setting, describe in two or three sentences what you believe Huck's reaction might be to the listed setting. Consider the details he would notice, the feelings he would have, and analogous situations from the novel that might support your ideas.

An English class in a modern American high school:

_____

_____

_____

_____

_____

Lunch at a McDonald's Restaurant:

_____

_____

_____

_____

_____

A video arcade in a modern shopping mall:

_____

_____

_____

_____

_____

Idea Checklist Activity (Elementary)

SCAMPER

A majority of students in your school have been complaining about their unsatisfactory lunch experiences. They seem to be unhappy with just about everything involving lunch—the food, the atmosphere, the cafeteria, the length of time. You have been chosen as a representative from your grade level to a committee that has been formed to improve your school's lunch-time. You will be using the SCAMPER technique to help you think about the lunch-time trouble in new ways and possibly to find some solutions to these pressing problems.

1. Spinach is a vegetable served on school lunches at least once a week. Very few children in your school ever eat the spinach. What other food might you substitute for spinach that most children would like while still having the same nutritional value? [Substitute]

2. What are some other things you might combine with lunch-time to make lunch a more pleasant experience? [Combine]

3. How could the present physical setting of the cafeteria be adapted to improve the lunch-time atmosphere? [Adapt]

4. Many students in your school do not like the portions of food they are served at lunch. What are some ways the food servings could be magnified or minified according to individual preference without having to increase the cost for food? [Magnify or Minify]

5. Much time is wasted at lunch when students finish eating. Students currently must simply sit quietly at their tables until the lunch period is over. What are some other possible uses for this time? [Put to other uses]

6. What are some elements of the lunch situation that could be eliminated to make lunch a more pleasant experience? [Eliminate]

7. How could the daily schedule be rearranged to give students and teachers more time to relax at lunch? [Rearrange]

Idea Checklist Activity (Secondary)

SCAMPER

SCAMPER is a type of idea checklist in which ideas are substituted, combined, adapted, modified, magnified, minified, put to other uses, eliminated, and rearranged. In the activity below, the SCAMPER technique is used to create questions that ask you to view the issue of life after high school in many different ways.

Exploring your desires, interests, and speculations about your options after high school can be helpful in making your future plans. In this activity, you will use divergent thinking to consider your life after high school. Simply answer the questions below. Remember, wild ideas are acceptable.

1. What occupational and educational advantages might a city with over 100,000 people offer over a much smaller city? [Magnify]

2. In what ways might going to a small college, rather than a large one, make it easier for you to make friends? In what ways might it be harder? [Minify]

3. What purposes, other than those which are strictly social or academic, do you think going to college serves? [Put to other uses]

4. What are some ways of furthering your education after high school that do not include going to a university? [Substitute]

5. What are some ways you might combine your occupation and education? [Combine]

6. What are some of the advantages and disadvantages to beginning your career before getting a college education? [Rearrange]

7. If your parents informed you that they would be unable to support you in any way after your high school graduation, in what ways might your plans be changed? [Eliminate]

Ground Rules for Convergent Thought

Convergent thinking allows the learner to refine and select among the ideas generated during divergent thinking. As with divergent thought, the specific techniques encouraging convergent thought are slightly different for each stage of creative problem solving, but Isaksen and Treffinger (1985) identify some very important ground rules upon which all the specific activities discussed later in this book are based. Again, students should keep these in mind as they progress through the convergent phases of each step.

- **Develop a Sense of "Affirmative Judgment"**—All the convergent activities offered in this book for evaluating ideas are designed to help spot strong ideas. The goal is to find good ideas, not slaughter bad ones.
- **Be Deliberate**—Develop and follow a specific plan for evaluating your ideas. This is not the time for arbitrary decisions. Convergent thought should be organized and logical.
- **Be Explicit**—It is essential that during the convergent phases of creative problem solving, you be completely "up-front" about your basis for evaluating ideas. This avoids the troubles that hidden agendas and unspoken preferences might bring to the process. Always be clear, honest, and specific throughout the convergent phases.
- **Avoid Premature Closure**—Don't stop evaluating until every idea has been given full and fair consideration. Sometimes groups want to "close-up shop" as soon as the first idea comes along. Don't allow this to happen. Continue the evaluation process until all ideas have been dealt with.
- **Take a Risk to Look at Difficult Issues or "Sneaky Spots"**— Be willing to deal with the most difficult issues early on. Don't simply avoid them. Rather, deal with them early so they don't become problems later.
- **Keep Your Eyes on Your Objective**—It is easy to move off track during the convergent phase; always keep your objective in mind.

The techniques below—musts & wants, hits & hot spots, evaluation grids, and ALU—help students achieve the above guidelines. While each can be used independently, these techniques may also be used in tandem. For example, in the musts & wants technique, students select the criteria they will use to evaluate a set of ideas, and hits & hot spots is used to narrow a list of ideas down to four or five so they will fit on the evaluation grid. Students then apply the criteria selected using musts & wants to the ideas chosen using hits & hot spots on an evaluation grid to select a most promising idea. Students may use ALU, another evaluation strategy, to choose between two strong ideas when a clear winner on the evaluation grid is not evident.

The convergent process has many applications to traditional classroom content. On the elementary level, evaluation techniques may be used in language arts to select a product to be developed for a book report. In science, students might use the process to determine the most promising experiment to test a particular hypothesis. Students in a social studies class might select a product to be marketed to raise money for a class purchase.

On the secondary level, the evaluation tools below might be used in an English classroom to select the author most representative of a movement in literature. In a history class, the students might select the political decisions made during the 1930s – 1940s which have the most impact on the American population in the 1990s. Students in a science classroom might use the process to select among various science fair project ideas. Essentially, students can employ this process in the classroom whenever they are asked to select among a number of ideas, issues, or concepts.

The following section offers a number of classroom activities designed to help illustrate some of the strategies or "tools" for thinking convergently. Like the divergent tools above, students use these convergent tools extensively during the creative problem solving process. Direct training in these strategies is important in the development of effective problem solvers.

Convergent Activities
Musts and Wants

If evaluation is to be effective, students must learn that at the heart of any well-formed evaluation or selection is a criterion for evaluation. Whether one is choosing a restaurant at which to eat, a television show to watch, or a sporting event to attend, one is basing a decision on criteria of some type. For example, when choosing a restaurant, the following might be the criteria used for evaluation:

• Will the restaurant's food taste good?
• Will the menu include some exotic or unique items?
• Will the atmosphere be pleasing?
• Will the prices be reasonable?

Of course, the trouble begins when one becomes unaware of the criteria for evaluation or selection being used. One easily slips into using criteria she might never choose to use if she were aware of her criteria for evaluation. For instance, in many cases, one's criteria for choosing a restaurant might become:

• Is it where I usually go to eat?
• Is the selection of meals what it usually is?

People are so often prone to habit or the "comfortable" that they can easily fall into the trap of making decisions based on the criterion of habit rather then making decisions based on the criteria that will lead to the best choice. By explicitly stating criteria for evaluation, one goes a long way in avoiding the problem of making the habitual choice rather then the best choice.

In the lesson that follows, students explore the idea that there are two types of criteria—*musts and wants* (Isaksen & Treffinger, 1985). The first type, *musts*, includes those criteria that the idea eventually chosen *must* meet. The second, *wants*, includes those criteria that the students *want* the idea to meet. For example, if a teenager has fifteen dollars for a Friday night activity of some type, then the activity she finally selects *must* cost less than fifteen dollars. "Does the activity cost less then fifteen dollars" is one example of a *musts* criterion. If the student *wants* the activity to involve many of her friends, then "Will the activity involve many of my friends" is one example of a *wants* criterion.

This distinction is rather important in that it gives students an effective "first line" method for choosing the strongest ideas from a long list. That is, after evaluating ideas to determine which ideas meet the students' musts criteria for evaluation, a long list of ideas would be reduced significantly.

One note of warning—understand that a musts criterion is based essentially on an assumption that overcoming the challenge that the musts criterion presents is not worth doing. For example, in the example above, our activity seeking student might have raised more money than the fifteen dollars available for her Friday night. The student simply made the decision not to do so. The decision to call a criterion a must is one that should not be taken lightly.

Like the other strategies in this book, musts and wants has many applications in both the elementary and secondary classrooms. Elementary students might consider which qualities political leaders must have to be effective and which qualities they would like political leaders to possess. Also, elementary students might discuss the characteristics which a "good" story written for their age group must have to be interesting for them and those characteristics they would like stories written for their age group to demonstrate.

On the secondary level, a science class might list the tools it must have in order to successfully complete a given science experiment and develop a list of tools that it would like to have available. In the English classroom, students might discuss the characteristics a particular literary work must possess in order to be a part of a literary movement such as Realism. Then the class could discuss other characteristics some authors of that movement demonstrated that were unique to the authors' styles (i.e., not typical of the movement).

Musts and Wants Activity (Elementary)

Rained Out

Due to the bad weather that you have been experiencing in your town lately, your class will have to spend recess in the classroom for the next several days. You need to decide upon an activity that can be done in the classroom during recess.

You want your recess activity to be fun and to be a break from your school day routine, but there are three criteria you *must* meet when selecting an acceptable activity:

- The activity must be safe. Therefore, it cannot involve any action that might result in injury or damage to the classroom.
- The activity must be quiet enough not to disturb surrounding classes.
- All students in the class must be able to participate in the activity.

The class has already brainstormed several ideas for possible activities. These ideas are listed below. Look through the list and circle the ideas that you believe will meet all three "musts" criteria listed above.

- Watch a video
- Play Red Rover
- Do art projects
- Play Seven Up
- Play Hangman
- Do extra math worksheets
- Play Freeze Tag
- Listen to music
- Play kick-ball
- Play spelling or math bingo
- Play I Spy
- Each child decides individually what to do
- Have a rest period with heads down on your desks
- Sing and play musical instruments
- Read silently from a book of your choice
- Play dodge-ball

Musts and Wants Activity (Secondary)

Class Vacation

For the last few years, you and your classmates have raised money in hopes of taking a one-week trip together. As students in a small Texas town, your fund raising has gone slowly, but you have raised quite a bit of money for your vacation over the last few years.

While you want your vacation together to be fun, involve many social activities, and take you to an exotic or unusual place, you know that any idea you eventually choose *must* meet the following criteria:

* Will it cost less than $400.00 per person? (This is the amount you have raised divided by the number of students in your class—you have made the decision to require no one to spend any of their personal money to take this trip.)
* Can we finish the vacation in less then a week? (Many students have jobs and other plans that will not allow them to be gone longer than a week.)
* Does the activity have educational value? (To go on this trip, you will need school sponsors and parent support. The only way to gain both is to select a trip that offers some educational value.)

For weeks, the student council has been gathering vacation ideas. Many of these ideas are listed below. Look through the list and circle the ideas that you believe will meet the three *musts* criteria for evaluation listed above.

* Dude Ranch; 130 miles; Bus

* Cruise to Bahamas or Caribbean; 1600 miles; Airline & Ship

* Glass Bottom Boat at Aquarena Springs (San Marcos, TX); 40 miles; Bus & Boat

* Beach; 400 miles; Bus or Airline

* Historic Jamestown (Revolutionary Period Town), VA; 900 miles; Bus or Airline

* Food & Architecture of New Orleans, LA; 500 miles; Bus or Airline

* Zoo, Sea World, Beach of San Diego, CA; 1000 miles; Bus or Airline

* Epcot Center (Orlando, FL); 800 miles; Bus or Airline

- New York Excursion; 1200 miles; Bus or Airline

- Windjammer Cruise in Jamaica; 1500 miles; Airline

- South American Excursion; 4000 miles; Airline

- Mexico City; 1500 miles; Airline

- Quarter Horse Championship; 250 miles; Bus

- Middle Ages Festival & Plays; 250 miles; Bus

- San Antonio, TX (Historic Hispanic culture, River Walk, and Sea World); 300 miles; Bus or Airline

- Tubing & Riding Rapids in New Braunfels, TX (includes German culture and foods); 250 miles; Bus

Musts and Wants (Secondary—English)

A Romantic Representative

During the period 1840 – 1865, the Romantic movement in America acted as a powerful force in literature. Authors such as Hawthorne, Melville, Thoreau, and Whitman shared, through their art, a new vision of truth and purpose in literature. While each of the authors of this period was unique, certain characteristics of their works were similar. These similar characteristics include:

1. An exploration of exotic settings or reactions to those settings
2. An emphasis on nature—the natural world—as a source of truth
3. A preference for feeling or emotion over reason and logic

The list below is composed of many works by American Romantic authors. Determine the works which are most representative of the Romantic movement by circling the works which contain *all three* of the characteristics listed above—that is, to be representative, a work *must* contain all three characteristics. Of course, all of the works listed below are characteristic of the Romantic movement, but your job is to find those that are most representative. You may find it necessary to review or reread some selections before working this activity.

"Rip Van Winkle" by Washington Irving

"To a Waterfowl" by William Cullen Bryant

"The Chambered Nautilus" by Oliver Wendell Holmes

"Nature" by Ralph Waldo Emerson

"The Rhodora" by Ralph Waldo Emerson

Walden by Henry David Thoreau

The Scarlet Letter by Nathaniel Hawthorne

Song of Myself by Walt Whitman

"I Hear America Singing" by Walt Whitman

"I Never Saw a Moor" by Emily Dickenson

Hits and Hot Spots

In their book *Creative Problem Solving: The Basic Course*, Isaksen and Treffinger (1985) outline an effective technique for identifying the strong ideas from a list. This technique, called hits and hot spots, involves three steps. First, a group of students reviews a list of ideas one item at a time. As an item is reached, students in the group can either remain silent or, if the idea strikes them as having merit, they can call out, "hit." Any student in the group can call an idea a hit, and students may call as many ideas as they wish hits. If any student calls an idea a hit, it is circled. Using this technique, it is easy to identify the stronger ideas on a list. This technique is a very efficient method for reducing the number of ideas on a list by half—a real need when the list exceeds fifty ideas.

The second step in the process involves categorizing ideas into "hot spots." A hot spot is simply an area where a number of ideas seem to cluster. For example, when asked to list the problems adolescents face, a group of teenagers listed a number of ideas. Using "hits," the group narrowed their list to the items below:

- acne
- transportation
- getting a car
- parents' unreasonable expectations
- getting a license
- buying clothes
- buying make-up
- arguments with parents

To find the hot spots, students reviewed their list beginning with the first idea. Because idea number one is obviously part of the first category of ideas (as yet, no other categories exist), a number one is written to the side of that idea. Next, students moved to idea two, "transportation," and asked, "Is this a new category or could this fall into category one?" Clearly, transportation is a new category, so a number two was placed to the side of that idea. Next, the group moved to the third idea, "getting a car," and asked, "Is this idea a new category, or could this fall into category one or two?" This idea seemed to relate to category number two, so a number two was written to the side of that idea. This process continued until all ideas on the list were assigned a number.

1. acne
2. transportation
2. getting a car

3. parents' unreasonable expectations
2. getting a license
1. buying make-up
1. buying clothes
3. arguments with parents

Once all ideas were assigned categories, the students assigned titles to the categories. Titles describe the critical attribute of the category—the attribute that distinguishes it from the other ideas. The title should be general enough to include all items assigned to the category, and it should be specific enough to exclude items in other categories. The group of students assigned category titles as follows:

Personal Appearance
1. acne
1. buying clothes
1. buying make-up

Transportation
2. getting a car
2. getting a license
2. transportation

Strained Relationships with Parents
3. arguments with parents
3. parents' unreasonable expectations

In the activities below, students use hits and hot spots to narrow a list of good ideas. Essentially, anytime students need to quickly narrow a long list, hits and hot spots may be used. In the elementary classroom, students might narrow a list of questions they have developed in preparation for a unit on far-away locations. Also, they might use the strategy to narrow a long list of insects they have observed. This list could be narrowed down to a few hot spots from which the students would choose one for an independent study project.

On the secondary level, students might narrow a list of various research topic ideas related to the Middle Ages. Further, secondary students in a math class might use hit & hot spots to identify, from a previously generated list, the strategies and information they will need to solve a particular geometric proof.

Hits and Hot Spots Activity (Elementary)

A boy in your class, Ryan, has been causing many problems for you, your classmates, and your teacher. Because no one in the class—including Ryan—is able to devote him or herself to school work due to Ryan's unruly behavior. The class has decided to work together to help Ryan solve his problems. Your desire is to make your classroom a more pleasant and productive place.

Below is a list of many of the problems caused by Ryan. Use the technique of hits and hot spots to focus this list to determine the most important problems that need to be addressed. Remember, hits and hot spots is a three step process:

1. Circle all ideas that you consider "hits" (of interest, value, or importance).
2. Use a separate sheet, and group the circled ideas into categories of ideas using the hot spots technique (ask your teacher if you need a review of this technique).
3. Create titles or names for each of the categories in which you have grouped ideas.

- Ryan frequently hits or pinches other children.
- The teacher must spend much time correcting Ryan.
- Ryan does not sit still in his seat.
- Ryan blurts out answers to questions without letting other students answer.
- Many students are afraid of Ryan.
- Ryan rarely finishes his school work.
- Other students have trouble concentrating on their work because Ryan is constantly making noises and talking loudly.
- Even though he is very smart, Ryan is in danger of failing this year because he does not turn in his school work.
- Ryan talks back to the teacher and argues with her.
- Fights often occur on the playground because of Ryan's treatment of other children.
- Ryan takes things off other children's desks and tears them up.
- Other children refuse to play with Ryan at recess or sit by him at lunch.
- The teacher often becomes angry with Ryan because she has to correct him so often.

Hits and Hot Spots Activity (Secondary)

A Kinder & Gentler School

Elections for president of the student council are two weeks away. Your best friend, Yolanda Martinez, is planning to run for the position. However, she is concerned about her speech to the student body. In the speech, she wants to address issues important to students at the school. Yolanda has given your group a list of problems, concerns, and challenges which she has either felt herself or heard others at school discuss.

She has asked your group to help her focus this list—to narrow it down to the issues most important to the student body. Use the technique of hits and hot spots to focus this list:

1. Circle all ideas that you consider "hits" (of interest, value, or importance).
2. Use a separate sheet, and group the circled ideas into categories of ideas using the hot spots technique (ask your teacher if you need a review of this technique).
3. Create titles or names for each of the categories in which you have grouped ideas.

- Classrooms are drab and colorless
- Lunch has no variety
- Poor student involvement at school functions
- Lockers get jammed
- Writing and graffiti on lockers
- Little spirit at the school
- Hallways are too crowded
- Bulletin boards in some classrooms never change
- Too much noise in the lunchroom
- Fights after school
- Lunch food is drab and boring
- Teachers who don't have time for you
- Teacher who are rude or don't respect you
- Students who are prejudiced
- Students who make fun of others
- Same menus served over and over in the cafeteria
- Students who don't care about anything

Hits and Hot Spots Activity (Secondary—Social Studies)

An Issue of War

The American Civil War forced the people of an entire nation into a deadly turmoil. The resolution of this war came after four bloody years of fighting (1861 – 1865). During that time, the United States faced many issues.

This activity acts as a preliminary stage in a research project. During this stage you will explore many of the possible topics for a research paper on the Civil War. To get your topic ready for exploration, you will need to consider some of the important issues of the period. Focus the list of possible topics below by using the technique of hits and hot spots.

1. Circle all ideas that you consider "hits" (of interest, value, or importance).
2. Use a separate sheet, and group the circled ideas into categories of ideas using the hot spots technique (ask your teacher if you need a review of this technique).
3. Create titles or names for each of the categories in which you have grouped ideas.

- Battle Field Surgery

- Hand-to-Hand Combat

- Expectations of Women's Behavior

- Social Events and Customs

- Exceptional Achievements by Females

- Exceptional Achievements by African-Americans

- African-American Spirituals

- Asian-American Involvement in Railroad Construction

- Character Traits of Effective Civil War Generals

- Differences in Southern and Northern family life

- Propaganda During the War

- Treatment of Differently-Abled Americans after the War

- Medical Technology and Practice During the 1800s

- Social Events and Customs Among Adolescents

- African-American Involvement in the War

- The Roles Individuals were Expected to Play in the Family

- Factory Technology and Production

- The Dynamics of the Southern and Northern Economies

- Anti-War Protests During the War

- Family Finances During the War

- Attitudes and Opinions of the Population Toward the War

Evaluation Grid

Treffinger and Isaksen (1985) outline the use of the evaluation grid. The grid is a powerful tool for evaluating a smaller number of ideas (usually, three to seven ideas). The technique requires four steps. First, students choose the criteria with which they will evaluate a set of ideas. They then list their criteria across the top of the grid. For example, if a group of students were evaluating ideas for a school party, one criterion might be, "To what extent will it be fun for students?" Another criterion might be, "To what extent will it be safe?"

Students would then list these criteria along the top of the evaluation grid (see Figure Two). Next, students list the ideas to be evaluated down the left side of the grid. For example, students might list a casino party, a dance, or even a medieval festival. Third, *progressing one entire column at a time*, students evaluate the ideas listed. For example in grid below, students found the idea of a casino party most fun (ranking it number one), a dance less fun (ranking it number two), and a medieval festival least fun (ranking it a number three). As the students progressed, they completed one criterion's column before moving to the next.

Evaluation Grid

Ideas	Fun CR 1	Safe CR 2	Inexpensive CR 3	Unique CR 4	Acceptable to all involved CR 5	TOTAL
Dance	2	3	1	3	2	11
Casino Party	1	2	2	2	3	10
Medieval Festival	3	1	3	1	1	(9)

Figure Two

Once students have evaluated all criteria for all ideas, the rows (across) are totaled. The idea with the lowest total is the idea that bears the most promise. In the case of Figure Two, the medieval festival idea scored lowest and thus was selected.

A few words of caution are in order. First, if an idea seems very strong, but fails to score lowest because it is weak on one criterion, students may wish to make modifications to that idea so that it will score higher. If fact, there is no reason that this process of modification cannot be applied to any idea at any point in the evaluation process.

Second, always word criteria in the same direction. That is, the criteria, "Will it be fun" and "Will it be inexpensive" are worded in the same direction—a ranking of one (1) would mean the same for each. "Will it be fun" and "Will it be too expensive" are not worded in the same direction—a ranking of one (1) would be positive in the first case and negative in the second. The totaled scores will be meaningless unless all criteria are worded in the same direction.

Third, students are ranking ideas (1, 2, 3, 4, and 5), they are not rating them (1, 2, 2, 3, 1). For this reason, two ideas will never receive the same rank for a given criterion. Finally, small groups should try to work for consensus when giving each idea a rank.

The evaluation grid acts as an effective tool for students in both elementary and secondary classes. An elementary teacher might ask students to evaluate various types of government after a study of governments from around the world. Or, an elementary teacher might ask students to evaluate some of the stories they have read during a unit of study.

On the secondary level, a social studies teacher might ask a class to evaluate the effectiveness of British monarchs during the 16th and 17th centuries. A math teacher might ask students to evaluate various products using the evaluation grid and math concepts. For example, using an evaluation grid, students might determine the "best" popcorn by analyzing such items as the proportion of kernels popped to the cost of the popcorn, the flavor, and the volume of popped kernels. Of course, as any good scientist knows, a hands-on experiment will be the only way to determine the scores the various brands of popcorn will receive.

Evaluation Grid Activity (Elementary)

Teacher's Pet

Your class has decided to get a classroom pet. The teacher and principal have agreed to allow you to purchase a pet, but there are several items you must consider before choosing a particular animal. First, the pet must be paid for by the students. Neither the school nor your teacher will contribute any money for the animal or for its lodging. However, the school will provide food for the animal throughout the school year.

Also, you must be completely responsible for the care and feeding of the animal. Although food will be provided, neither the teacher nor any other school personnel will assume any responsibility for feeding the pet or for keeping it healthy and clean. Remember that people are only in the school building for five days a week. Keep in mind how the pet will be cared for over the weekend. Additionally, each student in the class should have equal responsibility for the pet.

Third, when choosing a pet, you will need to keep in mind the safety of the pet as well as any dangers it might pose to the people around it. For example, an animal that needs a cold climate would not be very safe in a south Texas classroom. On the other hand, a poisonous snake would threaten the safety of its caretakers. Not only must your classmates' safety be considered, their personal preferences should also be taken into account. Some students might be allergic to particular animals, afraid of them, or simply dislike them for one reason or another. Every child in the class should be happy with the pet that is chosen. These, as well as many other ideas, should be considered to choose the perfect pet for your class.

1. Now that you are aware of the situation, brainstorm as many possible classroom pets as you can think of that your class might purchase. Use a separate piece of paper to record your brainstormed ideas. After brainstorming, you will probably want to do research on each animal on the list to find out more about them.

2. Next, develop five criteria by which to judge the pets you have suggested to choose the best one. Remember to state each criterion in the same direction.

3. From your brainstormed list and as a result of your research, choose five animals to consider as possible class pets and list them on the grid. Write your five criteria across the top of the grid. Complete the grid according to directions given by your teacher.

Criterion 1:

Criterion 2:

Criterion 3:

Criterion 4:

Criterion 5:

Evaluation Grid Teacher's Pet						
Animals	CR 1	CR 2	CR 3	CR 4	CR 5	TOTAL

Evaluation Grid Activity (Secondary)

For the Common Good

History

In the winter of 1994, a German scientist announced that he had discovered a process for ending human aging. When the process was performed upon a human zygote (the earliest developmental stage of a fetus), the resulting individual would live a life free from the effects of old age. While most of those treated would eventually die from disease or accident, their average life spans would still be over 400 years.

While the news sounded exciting at first, governments began to worry. At the time, the world's population stood at over 5.7 billion and was increasing by almost 90 million a year. In an already crowded world, the idea of unleashing a process that prevented death by aging was frightening. Such a process foretold a horrible future. Under such conditions, shortages of food, clean water, energy, and other resources would reach crisis proportions. Human life would be little more than a cramped, joyless existence.

Fearing such a future, world leaders acted. Acting through the United Nations, the leaders of the world established the Council for Genetic Control (CGC). The CGC was given control of the new genetic technique, and the sole authority to determine who should receive the treatment. As the process has to be performed on a human zygote, the only way for the CGC to make such a decision is to evaluate the parents of the potential offspring. The United Nations granted each of its member-nations a branch of the CGC with specific quotas based on population, available resources, and other relevant factors.

The American CGC is limited to choosing only 100 couples a year. In a complicated process repeated 100 times each year, CGC computers pick five promising couples from those who have applied. The information provided by these couples is then used by the American CGC to choose a single couple from the five who will be allowed to have an ageless child.

Because ageless humans may bare children throughout their long lives, a single individual might be responsible for fifty or more children. Clearly, in the distant future, a majority of the human race may be able to trace its lineage back to the couples picked by the CGC. The choices the CGC makes are very important.

Instructions

In this simulation, you and your classmates play the part of members of the American CGC. To make the best decision possible, you will meet in a small group and choose five criteria for evaluating the five couples' applications (list these on the bottom of page 57). You will then use an evaluation grid (page 57) as a group to evaluate the couples and choose one whose child may receive the new process.

Couple 1

Wife's Name: Maria L. Benavides
Occupation: Free-lance Photographer
Age: 24
Intelligence: Above Average
Race: Hispanic
Education: BA in Journalism
Goal: Own and run a photography studio
Medical Background: Maria is an excellent athlete who was involved in many high school sports.
Personal Information: Maria is a highly creative person whose work in photography is highly valued. She is also actively involved in environmental issues and has recently become interested in local politics.
Husband's Name: Benjamin Benavides
Occupation: Computer Programmer
Age: 25
Intelligence: Above Average
Race: Hispanic
Education: BS in Computer Science
Goal: Own and run his own software company
Medical Background: Ben's father died of heart disease at 38, and his mother developed terminal cancer at age 56.
Personal Information: Ben is a highly motivated computer programmer. Because of his exceptional, almost genius, skills in math and computer programming, he is highly valued by his present employer.

Couple 2

Wife's Name: Veronica Ladd
Occupation: Newspaper Reporter
Age: 25
Intelligence: Above Average
Race: Black
Education: BA in Journalism
Goal: Become a reporter for a major daily newspaper
Medical Background: Veronica is a carrier of sickle–cell anemia. While she does not suffer from the disease, there is a *small* chance that her children will.

Personal Information: Veronica is a very good reporter with whom her superiors are impressed. She enjoys her job and is involved in a number of community activities.

Husband's Name: Mark Ladd
Occupation: Lawyer
Age: 33
Intelligence: Above Average – Genius
Race: Black
Education: Law degree
Goal: Become a U.S. senator
Medical Background: Mark is an exceptional athlete who played on tennis and soccer teams in both high school and college.
Personal Information: Mark is a well respected and well liked individual. He has argued a case before the Supreme Court. Many fully expect him to realize his goals and, perhaps, exceed them.

Couple 3

Wife's Name: Joanne Lau–Peck
Occupation: Founder and Owner of Quest Toys, Inc.
Age: 30
Intelligence: Above Average – Genius
Race: Asian
Education: MBA in Marketing and Administration
Goal: Make Quest Toys America's largest manufacturer of children's toys
Medical Background: None Relevant
Personal Information: Joanne has a very strong, assertive personality. She is generally liked and respected by those who work with and for her. No one doubts that Joanne will achieve her goals.
Husband's Name: Jim Peck
Occupation: Department Store Manager
Age: 27
Intelligence: Average – Above Average
Race: White
Education: BBA in Management
Goal: Become a vice–president of the department chain for which he works
Medical Background: Jim's grandfather and uncle both died of heart disease.
Personal Information: Jim is a "people person." He enjoys working with others, and they enjoy working with him.

Couple 4

Wife's Name: Jan Weaver
Occupation: District Manager for a National Fast Food Franchise
Age: 24
Intelligence: Average – Above Average
Race: White
Education: High School Graduate
Goal: Jan would one day like to begin a home based mail–order business. She believes that by doing this she could have children and stay at home without sacrificing a second income.
Medical Background: Jan's family has a history of cancer of the reproductive organs.
Personal Information: Jan sees herself as a leader. She is highly valued by the company she works for because she has a natural ability to settle arguments and disputes among employees to everyone's satisfaction.
Husband's Name: Jack Weaver
Occupation: Foreman at Large Industrial Plant
Age: 23
Intelligence: Average
Race: White
Education: High School Graduate and Taking Night Classes at a Local Community College
Goal: Move into a management position at his company
Medical Background: Jack is in perfect health. At his high school, he played football and baseball and has managed to retain his physical fitness.
Personal Information: Jack enjoys people. Many of those who work under him at the factory see him as a true leader who will one day rise to powerful positions of leadership. He spends some of his free time coaching little league football and baseball teams.

Couple 5

Wife's Name: Anna Reynolds
Occupation: Physics Professor
Age: 27
Intelligence: Above Average
Race: Hispanic
Education: Ph.D. in Physics
Goal: Become head of physics department at her university and move the department toward more innovative research and teaching
Medical Background: None Relevant

Personal Information: Anna has some very innovative ideas about the science of physics. The most important of which is that she would like to see physics on the college and high school level taught in a more interesting and valuable way to more people. She wants the American population to understand, as she does, how exciting science can be.

Husband's Name: Randy McCabe

Occupation: Biology Professor

Age: 28

Intelligence: Above Average

Race: White

Education: Ph.D. in Biology

Goal: Randy loves the life of a research scientist. If given the chance, he would like to spend the rest of his working life researching in the laboratory and raising children with his wife.

Medical Background: Randy's father, a heavy cigarette smoker, died of lung cancer at age 49. Randy also smokes but says he wants to quit.

Personal Information: Randy is absorbed by his work. Though he is a loving and supportive husband, his real joy in life revolves around the discoveries he makes in the laboratory. Randy is a solemn individual who does not care for the company of more than a handful of friends.

List your criteria for evaluation:

Remember, each of the criterion below should begin with the phrase
"To what extent ..."

Criterion 1:

Criterion 2:

Criterion 3:

Criterion 4:

Criterion 5:

Evaluation Grid For the Common Good						
Couples	CR 1	CR 2	CR 3	CR 4	CR 5	TOTAL

Evaluation Grid Activity (Secondary—Science)

Environmental Impact

A concern for the way our society uses and protects the environment has grown in recent years. In this activity, you and your group will explore some of the ways humans impact the environment.

The purpose of this activity is to have your group identify the most destructive influence on the environment in your community. There are four steps to this activity. Follow the directions for each step below.

1. Identify a list of four destructive local influences on the environment. These influences might include automobile emissions, burning of trash, cleaning chemicals poured down drains, etc. If you generate more than four influences, use the technique of hits and hot spots to narrow your list (ask your teacher for more information if you are unfamiliar with the hits and hot spots technique).
2. Gather data about the various influences on the environment listed below. Answer each question listed below each influence. Remember, you should answer each question as it relates to the environment of your community, not as it relates to the global environment. You may gather data using any method you choose.

Influence 1: _____

Of what benefit is this influence?

Who benefits most from this influence?

How does this influence effect the environment?

What is the short-term negative impact of this influence on the local environment?

What is the long-term negative impact of this influence on the environment?

Influence 2: _____

Of what benefit is this influence?

Who benefits most from this influence?

How does this influence effect the environment?

What is the short-term negative impact of this influence on the local environment?

What is the long-term negative impact of this influence on the environment?

Influence 3: _____

Of what benefit is this influence?

Who benefits most from this influence?

How does this influence effect the environment?

What is the short-term negative impact of this influence on the local environment?

What is the long-term negative impact of this influence on the environment?

Influence 4: _____

Of what benefit is this influence?

Who benefits most from this influence?

How does this influence effect the environment?

What is the short-term negative impact of this influence on the local environment?

What is the long-term negative impact of this influence on the environment?

3. Identify four criteria you will use to determine the most destructive influence on your local environment. Your criteria should begin with the stem, "To what extent ..." For example, if your community has a land fill, a criterion on your list might be, "To what extent will the influence increase the amount of toxic substances in the land fill?" If clean air is an important issue, another might be, "To what extent does the influence harm the community's air quality?"

List your criteria for evaluation:

Criterion 1:

Criterion 2:

Criterion 3:

Criterion 4:

Criterion 5:

4. Use the evaluation grid below to identify the most damaging influence on your local environment. List the influences you identified on the left side of the grid, and evaluate them using the criteria you identified in step three.

Evaluation Grid Environmental Impact						
Influences	CR 1	CR 2	CR 3	CR 4	CR 5	TOTAL

ALU (Advantages, Limitations, Unique Potential)

ALU, as outlined by Treffinger and Isaksen (1985), is a convergent technique used to select between two strong ideas. The technique allows students to take an in-depth look at the A—advantages, L—limitations, and U—Unique Potential of each idea with which they are working.

The first step in the process requires that students focus on one of the two ideas. Students then list the various advantages which that idea promises. Next the group lists the idea's limitations, and finally, the group chooses a single unique potential that the idea possesses which the other idea does not. The group then repeats the process with the other idea.

For example, if students were evaluating two methods of studying, studying alone or with friends, the students might first examine the advantages, limitations, and unique potential of studying alone. Advantages might include increased concentration and few distractions. The limitations might include lack of feedback and limited availability of tutoring. The unique potential might be determined to be the fact that the individual controls the rate of study. Once the group lists the above ideas and others, the group's attention turns to the idea of studying in a group. At this point the group would repeat the ALU process, listing the advantages, limitations, and unique potentials of studying in a group.

Once the group has completed ALU, they can return to their original criteria (or generate criteria for evaluation if they have not done so). The students then evaluate the two ideas by assessing the degree to which the result of ALU for the ideas meets the group's chosen criteria.

A discipline-specific activity has not been provided for this strategy. ALU can easily be adapted for any situation in which students are asked to evaluate two ideas. On the elementary level, students might use ALU to determine the best course of action for a character in a story. Or, a class might use ALU to evaluate the contributions of two political leaders such as George Washington and Abraham Lincoln. One the secondary level, students might use ALU to evaluate the economic policies of front-running presidential candidates. Or they might use ALU to determine the most effective ideas for a science fair project.

ALU Activity (Elementary)

Your class has decided to do some type of project involving a local nursing home. You have already used an evaluation grid to determine your two best project possibilities. You will now need to use the evaluation technique of ALU to select the one best project.

The first project is called "Adopt-A-Grandparent." If you choose this project, each student in the class will "adopt" one particular resident of the nursing home. Your class will go to the nursing home as a group so that each student will have the opportunity to meet his or her adopted grandparent. At least once a month, you will be provided an opportunity in class to write a letter to your adopted grandparent and to make some type of gift to send along with the letter. Your teacher will make sure that all the grandparents receive their letters and gifts monthly.

The second project would not involve forming individual relationships with particular residents but instead would focus on monthly visits to the nursing home by your whole class. Instead of sending letters and gifts, your class would visit the nursing home once a month for a part of a school day and spend time talking with the residents and perhaps providing some entertainment for them.

Both of these projects were chosen from a larger list based on the following criteria:

- In which project would the greatest number of students want to participate?
- Which project would involve the greatest number of nursing home residents?
- In which project would students likely continue their involvement even after the project is no longer organized by the school?

Use ALU by first evaluating the "Adopt-A-Grandparent" project. List the advantages of adopting a grandparent. Then list the limitations of that project. Finally, record the single unique potential "Adopt-A-Grandparent" offers over monthly visits to the nursing home. Then follow the same process for the idea of monthly visits. List its advantages, limitations, and unique potential. Once both ideas have been evaluated using ALU, return to the criteria listed above and select the idea whose advantages, limitations, and unique potential best meet the criteria listed above.

Adopt-A-Grandparent Project

Advantages
*

*

*

Limitations
*

*

*

Unique Potential
*

Monthly Visits to Nursing Home
Advantages

*

*

*

Limitations
*

*

*

Unique Potential
*

Circle the idea you chose after reviewing the results of ALU and the degree to which each idea meets the criteria for selection listed above:

Adopt-A-Grandparent

Monthly Visits to Nursing Home

ALU Activity (Secondary)

In the activity below, you will select between two ideas. Both ideas are strong ones and you will need to use the technique of ALU—advantages, limitations, and unique potential—to choose the strongest of the two.

Your school has made a commitment to provide some type of recreation project for teenagers in your community. After much thought, you have narrowed your choices of projects for accomplishing this objective to two. In the first, students from your school, with support from local business and social organizations, would build a teen center—a central location where games, food, and entertainment would be available to local teenagers. In the second, the students of your school would develop an activities calendar that would provide a number of dances, fairs, and other activities for teenagers to be conducted throughout the school year at your school.

These two ideas were selected from many using the following criteria for evaluation:

- To what extent could the project be completed within six – eight months?
- To what extent would the students at our school want to work on the project?
- To what extent would local teenagers be interested in participating in our project?
- To what extent could we raise the money for the project (through donations, door fees, etc.)?

Use ALU by first evaluating the teen center project. List the advantages of a teen center. Then list the limitations of a teen center. Finally, record the single unique potential the teen center offers over the activities calendar. Then follow the same process for the activities calendar. List its advantages, limitations, and unique potential. Once both ideas have been evaluated using ALU, return to the criteria listed above and select the idea whose advantages, limitations, and unique potential best meet the criteria listed above.

Teen Center Project

Advantages

-

-

-

Limitations

●

●

●

Unique Potential

●

Activities Calendar

Advantages

●

●

●

Limitations

●

●

●

Unique Potential

●

Circle the idea you chose after reviewing the results of ALU and the degree to which each idea meets the criteria for selection listed above:

Teen Center

Activities Calendar

Chapter 2
The Creative Problem Solving Process

The creative problem solving process is not one to be mastered quickly. Students should first learn to use the thinking tools presented in Chapter One. Then, as the students master the tools of divergent and convergent thinking, the teacher can introduce the use of those tools within the context of the creative problem solving process. This chapter focuses on the creative problem solving process.

Creative problem solving is a six-step process designed to help individuals productively address the problems and challenges around them. Isaksen and Treffinger (1985) identify these six steps.

- **Mess-Finding**—During mess-finding, students identify a general topic area ("mess") on which to apply the rest of the process.
- **Data-Finding**—During data-finding, students take an inventory of what they know, need to know, or would like to know about the selected mess.
- **Problem-Finding**—During problem-finding, students identify a single statement of a problem associated with the mess.
- **Idea-Finding**—During idea-finding, students identify the many possible ways they might address their identified problem.
- **Solution-Finding**—During solution-finding, students identify a set of criteria to evaluate their solutions and identify a single solution for their chosen problem.
- **Acceptance-Finding**—During acceptance-finding, students generate a plan of action designed to implement their solution.

The following section describes each step of the creative problem solving process as Isaksen and Treffinger (1985) define it. It is important to note that each step is divided into two stages—the divergent stage and the convergent stage. It is during the divergent stage that students generate many ideas and during the convergent stage that they evaluate those ideas. As mentioned in Chapter One, the divergent stage and the convergent stage should not intermix. Students should complete the divergent stage and then progress to the convergent stage.

Mess-Finding

During this step in the process the students identify and accept a challenge or "mess" with which to work. The purpose of this step is not to identify a problem to solve; rather, it is to identify a general topic area on which to apply the creative problem solving process.

Students identify messes by probing the challenges, opportunities, situations, or concerns that they face in their lives. They are very general in nature and can be stated briefly. Examples of messes include "getting fit," "getting better grades," "improving my appearance" or "improving the conditions at the school."

Treffinger (1990) provides an excellent list of the types of messes which interest secondary students. This list includes dating, peer pressure, dealing with parents, improving grades, seeming to be different, and an uncertain world future. Topics such as dealing with divorce, making new friends, family relationships, school rules, pets, sports, or vacations might interest elementary students.

At times, the mess with which the student needs to deal is clear for it may be the very reason one employs the process. For example, a student concerned about her poor grades might employ the creative problem solving process in an attempt to deal with her weak school performance. Knowing the mess before using the creative problem solving process is quite natural. Many models of creative problem solving combine mess-finding and the step that follows it, data-finding, into a single step called fact-finding (Parnes, 1977). This is not to say that mess-finding is an unimportant step. Quite the contrary, this step allows a creative problem solving group with unclear objectives to clarify the area to which they will apply their energies.

The mess-finding stage is an excellent point for the teacher to introduce a pre-chosen mess. Doing so will allow the teacher to focus the students' attention on a specific content. For example, a secondary English teacher might offer a mess similar to that faced by Huck Finn in *Huckleberry Finn*. A history teacher might offer a mess similar to that faced by Lincoln just prior to the beginning of the Civil War. The opportunity for students to address these issues on their own before examining the actual literature or history can be an effective teaching strategy. The activities in Chapters Three and Four of this book are examples of pre-defined messes.

Mess-Finding—Divergent Phase

Students may use many of the divergent strategies discussed in Chapter One of this book during the creative problem solving process, and they should keep in mind the ground rules for divergent thought.

The goal of mess-finding is to probe challenges, opportunities, situations, or concerns of the students. As they brainstorm ideas related to these subjects, students may want to consider a number of questions posed by Sidney Parnes (1976).

- What would you like to do, have, or accomplish?
- What do you wish would happen?
- What would you like to do better?
- What do you wish you had more time for? More money for?
- What more would you like to get out of life?
- What are your unfulfilled goals?
- What angered you recently?
- What makes you tense, anxious?
- What misunderstandings did you have?
- What have you complained about?
- With whom would you like to get along better?
- What changes for the worse do you sense in attitudes of others?
- What would you like to get others to do?
- What changes will you have to introduce?
- What takes too long?
- What is wasted?
- What is too complicated?
- What "bottlenecks" exist?
- In what ways are you inefficient?
- What wears you out?
- What would you like to organize better?

After an adequate time has been devoted to brainstorming, students should move to the convergent phase of the mess-finding step.

Mess-Finding—Convergent Phase

During the convergent stage, students evaluate the messes they have generated and identify a single mess upon which to apply the rest of the creative problem solving process.

Five important questions may be asked at this stage:

- To what extent do we have influence over this mess?
- To what extent are we interested in working with this mess?
- To what extent will addressing this mess require imagination?
- To what extent is this mess important?
- To what extent could we address this mess in the immediate future?

Ask students to visualize a rating system of one or two (one = great – good and two = good – poor) for each of the above questions . Messes with good ratings (i.e., high influence, high interest, etc.) would receive a rating of one, and messes with poor ratings (i.e., low influence, low interest, etc.) would receive a rating of two.

Considering each question one at a time, the groups should place a check mark or star by each mess that scores a one for that question. When all messes have been evaluated for that question, students move to the next question and place a check mark or star by each mess scoring a one for it. The process continues until all messes have been evaluated. At any time, students may modify or combine messes so that they receive higher scores. Students should select the mess with the highest number of check marks as the one with which the group will work.

Mess-Finding in Action

To illustrate the use of the creative problem solving process, this chapter will trace an eighth grade student, Jennifer, as she progressed through the creative problem solving process. During the divergent stage of mess-finding, Jennifer considered the many challenges and opportunities she faces. She listed such ideas as peer pressure, friendship, grades, too much school work, getting in trouble with her parents, too many restrictions at home, loosing weight, staying up too late doing home work, and dating.

During the convergent stage of the mess-finding step, Jennifer chose one of the messes she generated in the divergent stage. To do so, she used the convergent process described above. Improving her school performance received the most checks. She had a high interest in working on this area, had high influence over it, and believed that she could address the mess within a reasonable period of time. Thus, Jennifer decided that she would use improving her school performance as her mess.

Data-Finding

During data-finding, students fully explore the mess they have identified. While working within this step, students identify what they presently know and need to know about their mess before they move to identify the single problem that they will solve.

This step is important because it gives the groups a chance to explore the mess. It prevents the group from focusing on one aspect of the mess before they are ready to do so. Furthermore, it allows the group to return to mess-finding and select another mess if necessary.

This is an excellent point in the process to involve local experts with your students. After students generate a list of information they presently know and need to know about the mess, the teacher might ask experts from the community to visit the class and answer some of the students' questions. For example, if students were working with the pre-defined mess faced by Lincoln just before the Civil War, a local historian or college professor might be brought in to answer questions the students may have about Lincoln's situation.

Data-Finding—Divergent Phase

As students work through this step, they may generate as many as five different kinds of data.

- Information—Students identify concrete facts related to their mess.
- Impressions—Students identify beliefs or hunches they hold concerning their mess.
- Observations—Students identify sensory impressions related to their mess.
- Feelings—Students identify emotions they hold related to the mess.
- Questions—Students identify areas of uncertainty concerning their mess.

Generally, this step is much like that done by newspaper reporters as they investigate a story. The goal of this step is to explore questions relating to the who, what, when, where, why, and how of the mess. Students should make lists of everything they know or need to know about their mess.

After students have had a sufficient period of time to generate their data, they should move to the convergent phase of data-finding and evaluate their data.

Data-Finding—Convergent Phase

Evaluating the data generated in the divergent phase is a three-step process which Isaksen and Treffinger (1985) call "Hits, Hot Spots, and Critical Concerns" (see Chapter One). First, students should go through the data they generated and identify items they consider to be important—the "hits." Any items deemed important should be circled. If one individual in the group feels an idea is important, then it should be identified as a hit.

Next, students should group circled items together if they seem to relate to one another. These groupings are called "hot spots." When the groups are finished grouping hits, they should review their hot spots by orally discussing how the hits in each hot spot are related.

Last, the groups rate their hot spots as being either high priority (requiring immediate action), medium priority (requiring prompt action), or low priority (requiring no action in the immediate future). Ranking hot spots will help students use their data more effectively in later steps of the creative problem solving process.

Data-Finding in Action

Jennifer, the eighth grader working on the school performance mess, reached the data-finding stage and used divergent thinking to explore what she knows and needs to know concerning school performance. During this stage, she listed such items as:

Things I know:
- I lack time management skills.
- There are books on study skills and time management in the library.
- There is a course on study skills offered.
- Rick and Virginia, my friends, do very well in school.
- I am sharpest in the mornings.
- I like studying with others.
- The hours of 8:00 p.m. to 10:00 p.m. are usually free for me.

Things I Need to Know:
- What study skills do I lack?
- Does our school offer after school tutoring?
- How do I get into the study skills class?
- Are there others interested in working with me on this?
- Do the counselors have study skills information in their offices?

When Jennifer finished brainstorming, she used the technique of hits and hot spots to narrow and group her list of ideas. For example her "Things I Know" list was narrowed and grouped into such categories as: friends doing well in school, times I have free, resources available to me, ways I like to study, and study skill areas I would like to improve. Jennifer followed the same process with her "Things I Need to Know" list. Then, Jennifer ranked her hot spots in order of priority.

After using hits and hot spots to narrow and focus her list, Jennifer moved to the next step in the creative problem solving process—problem-finding.

Problem-Finding

During the problem-finding step, students identify a single, important problem associated with their mess. When John Dewey wrote, "A problem is half solved if it is properly stated," he captured the essence of the problem-finding step. This step offers a direction for all that will follow. Isaksen and Treffinger (1985) explain that problem statements in creative problem solving have four components—the "invitational stem," the "owner," the action verb, and the goal or object of concern.

So that the statement invites a solution and implies that many solutions are possible, we begin with the stem, "In what ways might …" To help the group recorders, students could abbreviate this phrase (IWWM).

Next, the group needs to establish an owner or actor for its problem statement. The problem statement also needs a single action verb. This is the action the group would like the owner to take. Last, the problem statement should contain the goal or object of concern. This is the thing on which the action will be taken.

Stem	Actor	Action	Object
IWWM	we	involve	our students in the problem solving process?

Problem-Finding—Divergent Phase

During the first part of the divergent phase, students generate as many possible problem statements as possible. It is a good idea at this stage to consider many possible actors, actions, and objectives. The data-finding results will be especially helpful during this stage.

To stimulate ideas further, Isaksen and Treffinger (1985) suggest students experiment with "key word variations." Using this process, they generate new problem statements by substituting synonyms for various parts of previously generated actions and objectives. For example, the problem statement could be changed by simply introducing synonyms for the action verb and object of concern in the original statement. For example, the problem statement above might become, "IWWM we increase the frequency of the creative behaviors of our students?" This process of "key word variation" will produce many new problem statements.

Parnes (1985) suggests another way to increase the number of problem statements that he calls "massaging." When using this process, the group will massage their problem statement by asking "why?" For example, a student might state a problem such as, "In what ways might I get a car?" The facilitator might ask, "Why do you want a car?" The student might say, "Because I need transportation to work." This could be stated as the problem statement, "In what ways might I get transportation to work?" The process of massaging problem statements can continue for quite some time and be very productive.

Problem-Finding—Convergent Phase

In their book *The Handbook for Creative Learning* (1982), Treffinger, Isaksen, and Firestien outline an effective method for evaluating problem statements. This process, called "Highlighting," is very similar to the process of "Hits, Hot Spots, and Critical Concerns" discussed earlier.

First, students look though their list of problem statements and identify those problem statements that they consider to be of particular importance. "Hits" are marked with a check mark or star.

Next, the group identifies the "hot spots" by finding those hits that seem related. After the various hot spots have been identified, students should then try to phrase a problem statement for each hot spot that is general enough to encompass all the problem statements in the hot spot.

After all hot spots have been rephrased into more general problem statements, students may use one of two methods to identify a single, best problem statement. In the first, the group members will try to create a statement that is inclusive of all or many of the rephrased problem statements. When this is not practical, the various rephrased problem statements may be evaluated using the following criteria.

- Which problem statement lends itself to many possible ideas for solutions?
- In which problem statement are you most interested in generating ideas for solutions?

To get these two criteria to coincide with a single problem statement, it may be necessary to paraphrase or combine some of your problem statements.

At the end of the convergent phase of problem-finding, the group should have a single problem statement with which to work as they progress to the next step in creative problem solving.

Problem-Finding in Action

While working on this step, Jennifer first generated a number of problem statements. These included:

- IWWM I find a tutor for math?
- IWWM I learn more effective study skills?

- IWWM I learn to manage my time more effectively?
- IWWM I improve my performance in math and science?
- IWWM I raise my grades in math and science?

After generating a number of problem statements, Jennifer used the tools of convergent thinking to choose a single problem statement with which to work. She chose the statement: "IWWM I improve my grades in math and science?" Once Jennifer selected her problem statement, she moved on to the idea-finding step of the process.

Idea-Finding

During this stage of the creative problem solving process, students generate a number of possible ideas that address the problem statement. At this point, avoid calling the ideas generated "solutions." While many of the ideas generated may well act as solutions to the problem, other ideas will only be effective when used in tandem. To ask students only to generate complete solutions at this step in the process would eliminate many worthwhile ideas.

Idea-Finding—Divergent Phase

To begin the divergent phase of idea-finding, have the recorder of each group write the group's chosen problem statement on a piece of paper so that all can see it.

Parnes (1985) suggests that before the groups begin brainstorming, the facilitator explain that during the divergent stage of this step students should not ask questions about ideas generated. When individuals ask questions about ideas, Parnes explains, "they are really judging the appropriateness of a thought or idea. They may assume anything they want and just let ideas come. Later, during judging and selecting, the relevance can be assessed by the client or group." Parnes further suggests that you "urge the group to avoid 'editorializing'— that is, elaborating on an idea to justify it." This is simply not required during the divergent phase. There will be plenty of time for it later in the convergent phase of this step and the next. After offering these reminders, have the groups begin brainstorming ideas that address their problem statements.

It is important that groups really "stretch" during idea-finding. Groups need to move beyond simply brainstorming their known experiences to the generation of truly new and innovative ideas. This is not to say that verbalizing ideas from one's known experience is unimportant. Everyone's experiences are different and much can be gained from brainstorming at this level, but at some point the group will need to move to a higher level of brainstorming.

Isaksen and Treffinger (1985) offer a number of techniques for moving to this higher level. One of these suggestions is called "Attribute Listing." A group using this technique breaks the goal or objective of its problem statement down into its various "attributes." After writing each attribute down on a sheet of paper, the groups would consider each in isolation and offer ideas for improving it (see Chapter One for more details).

When each group has had plenty of time to generate ideas and has a number of intriguing ideas, it is time to move them to the convergent phase of idea-finding.

Idea-Finding - Convergent Phase

The convergent phase of idea-finding is similar to that found in other steps of creative problem solving. First, students should evaluate their ideas by circling or placing stars by the ideas they feel are "hits."

Next, if there is the need to reduce the number of ideas the group has to work with further, students should group related ideas together in "hot spots." Afterwards, they should paraphrase the hot spots in a manner general enough to include all the ideas in the hot spot.

Remind students that it is not the goal of this phase to single out one "best" idea. Rather, the groups should end this phase with a number of promising ideas that can then be effectively used in the next step of creative problem solving.

Idea-Finding in Action

Jennifer generated a number of ideas related to her problem, "IWWM I improve my grades in math and science?" during the divergent stage of idea-finding. These include:

- Develop a more organized evening study schedule
- Hire a tutor for after school
- Do my homework with Rick or Virginia
- Enroll in a commercial learning center
- Organize a study group of friends from my math and science class
- Ask my teachers for extra credit
- Drop those classes
- Take less advanced math and science classes
- Develop a weekly study schedule

Jennifer then used the convergent tool of hit & hot spots to narrow and refine her list down to four ideas:

- Organize a study group of friends from my math and science class
- Enroll in a local, commercial learning center
- Hire a tutor
- Develop a weekly study schedule

After narrowing her list to four, Jennifer moved to the next step in the creative problem solving process—solution-finding.

Solution-Finding

Solution-finding can be a bit confusing for many students because it is slightly different from the other steps in creative problem solving. The first goal of this step is to generate a set of possible criteria for evaluating the ideas generated in the last creative problem solving step.

The criteria a group generates will often take the form of "Will it ..." questions.

- Will it be inexpensive?
- Will it be implemented in a short period of time?
- Will it avoid abuses by ...?
- Will it be acceptable to ...?

Another way to phrase criteria is to use "To what extent will it ..." questions.

- To what extent will it be inexpensive?
- To what extent will it be implemented in a short time period?
- To what extent will it avoid abuse by ...?
- To what extent will it be acceptable to ...?

The latter method for phrasing criteria might be more appropriate for secondary students while younger students would do better with the former.

All groups should understand that criteria should be phrased in the "same direction." This means that a perfect solution should always receive the same answer to the criteria-questions. In "Will it ..." questions, a perfect solution would be answered with "Yes." In "To what extent will it ..." questions, the perfect solution would be answered with "To a great extent." Likewise, a very weak solution would receive answers of "No" in the "Will it ..." questions and an answer of "To a very limited extent" in the "To what extent will it ..." questions. By phrasing criteria in the "same direction," the groups can effectively use the evaluation grid discussed below and explained in Chapter One for the convergent phase of solution-finding.

After a number of possible criteria have been generated, the group evaluates the criteria and selects the most important. Next, the groups use the criteria to evaluate and select among the ideas identified in idea-finding.

Solution-Finding—Divergent Phase

Generating many possible criteria is the goal of this phase. Isaksen and Treffinger (1985) suggest that there are five general types of criteria—cost, time, feasibility, acceptability, and usefulness. For example, if a group has an established budget of $200, it might generate the cost related question of "Will it cost less than $200?"

One way to generate criteria which Parnes (1985) suggests is for students to look back over each of their strong ideas from the last creative problem solving step and ask "What is good about this idea?" and "What is bad about this idea?" Then, rephrase the answers to these questions into the form of criteria.

When the groups have fully stretched themselves and generated many possible criteria for evaluation, it is time to move to the convergent phase of solution-finding.

Solution-Finding—Convergent Phase

The convergent phase of solution-finding is broken into two parts. In the first, students identify only their strongest or most important criteria. In the second, they apply their criteria through evaluation and modification of their ideas.

Students should first evaluate their criteria by selecting the most important criteria. The groups may find that hits and hot spots may be effectively applied here as it was in other steps of the process. After students have identified a list of approximately five to ten criteria, they should separate their criteria into two groups—those criteria that their solution *must* meet and those criteria that they want their solution to meet.

This separation process is important because after a group has identified those solutions that meet their musts criteria, they can then modify those solutions to meet successfully their wants criteria.

Once a group's most important criteria has been separated into a list of musts and wants, it is time to evaluate ideas. Students evaluate their ideas on an evaluation grid (see Chapter One). The group lists its various ideas in the boxes on the right hand column of the grid, and list their musts criteria on the line running along the top of the grid.

Next, considering each criterion separately for all ideas (i.e., moving vertically down the columns before moving to the next criterion), the students rate their ideas from 1 to 5 (1 = best; 5 = poorest). It is important that the group consider all ideas for each criterion before moving to the next. In doing this, groups compare one solution with another for that criterion only.

After all ideas have been evaluated, the group should then total the scores for each idea in the column to the right. After the point scores are totaled, it should be clear which ideas offer the strongest potential. The idea with the lowest score is the idea which shows the greatest promise. However, even at this point, students my improve upon the "winning idea." A promising idea may be combined with others or modified to strengthen it further. Parnes (1985) explains, "the productive approach seems to dictate selecting these pet ideas and refining them, using the criteria as focal points to improve the ideas. For example, if an idea costs too much, develop ways to reduce costs."

Solution-Finding in Action

During this step, Jennifer generated a number of possible criteria. These included:

• To what extent will it allow me to work with others?
• To what extent can I fit it into my schedule?
• To what extent will it be enjoyable?
• To what extent will it motivate me to complete my homework?
• To what extent will it be inexpensive?
• To what extent will it have immediate results?
• To what extent will it offer long term benefits?

Jennifer identified her musts criteria:

• To what extent will it allow me to work with others?
• To what extent will it motivate me to complete my homework?
• To what extent will it be inexpensive?
• To what extent will it produce immediate results?

She then used the evaluation grid below to find her most promising idea. She evaluated her ideas by ranking each idea for each criterion on the grid. She was careful to complete one column before moving to the next (see Figure One).

Upon completing her grid, Jennifer noted that the idea of organizing a study group received the best score, a six. Based on this information, Jennifer decided that this would be the solution with which she would move to acceptance finding.

Evaluation Grid
Improving My Grades

Ideas	Work with Others CR 1	Motivational CR 2	Inexpensive CR 3	Immediate Results CR 4	Total
Study Group	1	1	2	2	(6)
Learning Center	2	3	3	3	11
Private Tutor	3	2	4	1	10
Study Schedule	4	4	1	4	13

Figure One

Acceptance-Finding

Isaksen and Treffinger (1985) outline the process to be used during the acceptance-finding step in creative problem solving. Students identify potential sources of assistance that will help implement their solution and potential sources of resistance that will hinder the implementation of their solution. After designing specific ways in which assisters may be used and resisters overcome, students design a detailed plan of action for the implementation of their solution.

Acceptance-Finding—Divergent Phase

Given any solution to a problem, there will always exist those people, places, and things that will help the implementation of the solution and those people, places, and things that will hinder the implementation of the solution. The purpose of the divergent phase of acceptance-finding is to identify both these assisters and resisters to a solution's implementation.

First, the group's recorder should draw a line down the middle of a sheet of paper. On the left side of the paper will be listed the assisters to the group's solution and on the right side will be listed the resisters. As the students brainstorm, they should consider all possibilities. Students should attempt to generate assisters and resisters for all the following categories—who, what, when, where, why, and how. Remind students that they should "stretch" to generate insights that they might have missed otherwise.

As students generate their lists, they may find that some assisters may also be identified as resisters. When an item falls on both the assister and resister list, students should consider it especially important.

After the group has generated its list of assisters and resisters, they should then review their list and circle those items that seem to be the most important. Once these items are identified and circled, the group should begin generating a list of actions that should be taken to effectively use the circled assisters and effectively overcome the circled resisters.

The items on a plan of action list should include three types of action.

- Action to be taken in the next twenty-four hours.
- Action to be taken soon.
- Action to be taken within a longer period of time.

The groups should keep in mind that they are still in the divergent phase of acceptance finding. They are brainstorming the various actions to be taken and thus generating a list of potential actions - not a complete plan.

Acceptance-Finding—Convergent Phase

The goal of this phase is to produce a specific plan of action that will implement the group's solution. The group should begin by identifying those actions that are important and separating those various actions into three categories—twenty-four hour actions, short-range actions, and long-range actions.

Once these actions are listed, students evaluate their plan using questions similar to those they used during mess-finding.

- Influence—Does your group have responsibility and decision-making authority within this plan?
- Interest—Is your group motivated to spend the time and energy necessary to put this plan into action?
- Imagination—Does your plan offer a new and unique way of dealing with your problem?

If the group answers "No" or is uncertain about the answers to any of the above questions, then it should modify its plan of action in such a way that it can answer "Yes."

Finally, the group should discuss any concerns it has about the implementation of its plan of action. These concerns should include the various things about the plan that might go wrong. After the concerns have been voiced and written down, the group should consider options for dealing with the concerns should they arise. Students should write down these options as well—knowing these will be important later as the group begins putting its plan to work.

Acceptance-Finding in Action

Jennifer began this step by considering the various resisters to and assisters of her solution. These included:

Resisters
- My schedule and my friends' schedules
- My friends—if they feel they aren't getting anything out of the sessions
- Afternoons—I have basketball practice
- Transportation
- Parents

Assisters
- Parents
- My big sister, Amy
- My teacher
- The hours of 8:00 – 10:00 p.m.
- My house for meetings

After using hits and hot spots to focus her list of resisters and assisters, Jennifer began writing a step-by-step plan for implementing her solution. Her plan attempted to overcome the significant resisters she identified and to use the significant assisters she identified.

Jennifer's Plan of Action

1. Get permission from Mom and Dad to have a weekly study group meet at our house.
2. Persuade Mom and Dad to help me make refreshments for each meeting.
3. Talk to three of my friends in my math and science classes who could help me and would be serious at the study sessions. Find out what their schedules are and find an evening during which we can work together.
4. Once I have three friends who can meet one evening a week, have Mom call their parents and let them know what we are doing. See if Mom can work out my friends' transportation.
5. Tell my teachers what I am doing and ask them to track any improvement I have over the next four weeks.
6. After four weeks meet with my teachers to determine if my solution is working.

A Few Suggestions for Teachers

Groups and Creative Problem Solving

Creative problem solving works well with groups of any size. Teachers introducing the process may wish to model the step as a whole group activities and later allow students to work through the process in small groups. However, when facilitating a large group the danger of some students "fading into the background" arises. To avoid this the facilitator may wish to help less verbal students by providing written divergent activities. For example, a facilitator might pose a question to the group, and then ask students to write down any ideas that come to them. After students have had time to brainstorm on paper, the facilitator can then ask for ideas orally.

Using Handouts & Activities

Early on, it is helpful to provide students not only with a full grounding in the creative problem solving process, but with structured activities such as those included in Chapter One, Three, and Four of this book. These activities are designed to help students master the process.

Keeping Out

As your students are working, do not interject your personal ideas and opinions. Remember, your job during the creative problem solving process is to keep groups moving and make sure that they are adhering to the ground rules for divergent and convergent thought. It is always tempting to mention some of your thoughts upon a subject to a group. But, remember that students are accustomed to classrooms where the teacher's opinions and views determine a class' focus and students' grade. In the eyes of some students, your ideas may hold more weight than the ideas of others students. Your interjected ideas will be inappropriately considered "better." Sidney Parnes states it best in *A Facilitating Style of Leadership* (1985), "When in doubt, leave it out!"

Using a Recorder

One individual should always record ideas as students think divergently and convergently at each step of the process. When facilitating an entire class, the teacher may act as recorder. When using creative problem solving with small groups, each group should appoint a recorder for its ideas. As groups may begin to generate ideas much faster than a single student can write, it is a good idea to appoint a back-up recorder. These two individuals can work in tandem to make sure all ideas are written down as soon as they are called out by group members. It is a good idea to rotate the job of recorder every now and then. This will allow everyone to share responsibility for this task. Also, all group members should keep a sheet of paper before them. Students can use this sheet to write down ideas coming too fast for the recorders.

Regardless of the size of the group, the recorder's work should be in plain sight of everyone. For a large group, large sheets of butcher paper may be required to record idea. For smaller groups, plain lined paper may be sufficient.

Chapter 3
Elementary CPS Activities

The authors designed the activities in this section to be used with elementary students. While the activities may be used separately, they may also be used in sequence. In the first activity, students explore the issue of heroes in literature (folk tales). In the second activity, they explore and evaluate the success of historical heroes. Finally, in the third activity, the students propose ways they might develop the qualities of their heroes within themselves.

Heroes in Folk Tales

Mess-Finding

Conduct this activity with a large group or whole class. Discuss with the group the fact that, in most fairy tales, bad things happen, but there are usually happy endings. The following questions might facilitate discussion:

- Why do you think bad things happen in fairy tales?
- Do they make the stories more interesting?
- Would the stories be better if only good things happened?

After the discussion, instruct students to think of all the fairy tales read and discussed in class and have them list all the bad or unpleasant things that happened in the stories. (You may want to specify particular fairy tales.) Record student responses on the board. After the brainstorming session, have students predict all the ways in which each story would be different if the unpleasant things had not happened. Again, record responses on the board.

Data-Finding

Conduct data-finding in a large group. Have students choose five fairy tales with which they are very familiar. (Again, you may wish to specify stories.) Working with one fairy tale at a time, have students identify the hero(s) or heroine(s) in each story. Then have them brainstorm all the good or admirable qualities of each hero or heroine as you record their responses. Finally, discuss how all the heroes or heroines are alike and how they are different. To compare and contrast their similarities and differences, make two columns on the board or chart tablet where you are recording. Label one "Likenesses" and one "Differences" and record and discuss students' responses.

Problem-Finding

Students may complete this step as a whole group or in small groups. If in a large group, students may vote on one of the five fairy tales discussed in Data-Finding to use for this step. In small groups, you may wish to assign a particular tale to each group. Have the group(s) list all the steps the hero had to go through or the obstacles he or she had to overcome to achieve a happy ending. You may need to act as recorder for all groups.

Idea-Finding

Working in the same group and with the same tales as in Problem-Finding, have students review their list of problems or obstacles and brainstorm other possible solutions the hero might have used to achieve a happy ending as you record their responses.

Solution-Finding

Students may continue working in the same small groups as they have previously. If they have been working in a large group, they will need to be placed in small groups at this time. Have each group rate their solutions from Idea-Finding on the rating scale provided. You may need to act as facilitator in the groups to ensure that each student participates and can justify their reasons for the rating of each solution. Groups will need to reach a consensus on their ratings, but not all groups (if they are working on the same tale) have to have the same rating for each solution.

Acceptance-Finding

For this step, students will need to work individually. Using the rating scale, students should choose one (or a combination of more) of the best solutions to the problems encountered in the fairy tale chosen in Problem-Finding. They will then each rewrite the fairy tales they have worked with but change the endings by having the heroes use their solutions instead of the solutions used in the original fairy tales. You may need to record students' stories as they dictate depending upon their writing skills. Students should present their completed stories to an audience in some fashion.

Solution Finding

Different Solutions a Hero Might Have Used

Idea Rating Scale
To rate each idea, circle a number on the 1 to 5 scale.

Possible Solutions:

Good ---------- Fair ---------- Poor

1. _____

   _____   1   2   3   4   5

2. _____

   _____   1   2   3   4   5

3. _____

   _____   1   2   3   4   5

4. _____

   _____   1   2   3   4   5

5. _____

   _____   1   2   3   4   5

6. _____

   _____   1   2   3   4   5

7. _____

   _____   1   2   3   4   5

8. _____

   _____   1   2   3   4   5

9. _____

   _____   1   2   3   4   5

10. _____

   _____   1   2   3   4   5

Choosing A Favorite Historical Hero

Mess-Finding

Students will carry out this step in small groups. Give each group the following instructions and provide a record sheet for each group. "We have studied about heroes in many different fields of knowledge throughout history. Men and women we consider heroes have made important contributions to science, government, exploration, education, and the betterment of lives of others in general. Many elements of our world have posed problems for people throughout time. Brainstorm the many worldwide problems that have existed throughout history."

Data-Finding

Students will carry out the rest of the steps individually. Instruct students to interview five people they know: parents, friends, brothers, sisters, etc. They will be asking the people they interview what they consider to be the biggest problems that have occurred in history, why these problems were particularly important, and the people they feel have made the most important contributions to society by helping solve those problems. These questions are included on the data-finding sheet provided, and you will probably want to discuss these questions with the students before their interviews. Each student will need five copies of the data finding sheet to record responses from their interviews.

Problem-Finding

In this step, students will be using the data they gathered during their interviews, as well as their own personal feelings, to choose what they feel is the most significant problem encountered in history. You will need to provide each student with a problem-finding sheet and go over the instructions with them.

Idea-Finding

Students may need to do further research at this step to learn more about people who have made contributions that have helped to solve the problem they chose in Problem-Finding. Provide students with the idea-finding sheet and go over the instructions with them.

Solution-Finding

Students will be working individually to choose five heroes within the context of the problems they chose. However, a large group discussion of developing criteria for evaluation might be needed here. Discuss with the class how to develop appropriate criteria to rank the contributions historical figures have made to society. Examples you might share would be "Benefited the most people" or "Had the most long-lasting effects," but be sure to let students suggest their own criteria also. Go over instructions for using the evaluation grid provided. Remind students to consider one criterion at a time for all five people they have chosen. Students may choose to use some of the same criteria developed through the class discussion, and this is acceptable at this point.

Acceptance-Finding

Present the acceptance-finding record sheet to your students and go over the instructions. In this final step, students will be elaborating upon the hero they have selected as making the most significant contribution to society by creating their own products that have been discussed and approved during individual conferences with you.

Mess-Finding

Historical Problems in Our World

_____

_____

_____

_____

_____

_____

_____

_____

_____

_____

_____

_____

_____

_____

_____

_____

_____

_____

_____

_____

_____

_____

_____

_____

_____

_____

_____

_____

_____

Data-Finding

Historical Problems in Our World

Interviewer_____

Person Being Interviewed_____

Question 1: What do you think is the biggest problem that has ever occurred in our world?

Question 2: Why was this problem so important?

Question 3: What person(s) contributed to solving this problem?

Problem Finding

The Most Important Historical Problem

I think _____ is the most

important historical problem because:

_____

_____

_____

_____

_____

_____

_____

_____

_____

_____

_____

_____

_____

_____

_____

_____

_____

_____

_____

_____

_____

_____

_____

Idea Finding

Heroes and Their Contributions

Using the problem you selected in Problem-Finding, list as many people as you can who have made important contributions toward solving that problem and what those contributions were.

Hero	Contribution
_____	_____
_____	_____
_____	_____
_____	_____
_____	_____
_____	_____
_____	_____
_____	_____
_____	_____

Solution Finding

Evaluating Historical Heroes

Ideas	CR 1	CR 2	CR 3	CR 4	CR 5	TOTAL
Evaluation Grid **Historical Heroes**						

Acceptance Finding

The Most Important Hero

The real-life, historical hero who received the most points on your grid should be the person you feel made the most important contribution to society. Develop a product that shows in detail who the person was and why the person was such an important hero. Discuss the specific requirements of your product with your teacher.

Name of Historical Hero: _____

Contribution to Society:

Why That Contribution Was Important:

Description of My Product:

Why I Chose This Product:

How Can I Develop Qualities of a Hero?

All the instructions for this activity are directed to the students.

Mess-Finding

Heroes are not perfect people. Many times, they are ordinary people—just like you—who have found themselves in extraordinary circumstances or who have performed extraordinary deeds. Their performance in such circumstances has caused them to be admired or respected. In most cases, heroes have possessed these admirable qualities all along but other people may have only recognized them under specific circumstances. *You* have the potential to be a hero.

You have positive qualities about yourself that could be developed further as well as negative qualities that could be changed for the better. Brainstorm all the attributes of your personality that you think could be improved—a little or a lot!

Data-Finding

Design a survey to distribute to ten of your friends. Each friend should respond to the survey by telling what they like best about you and what they like least about you. This will help give you a realistic picture of how others see you. While their answers might not make you feel very good at first, remember that the purpose of this activity is to help you become the best person you can be!

Problem-Finding

To improve anything, we have to move one step at a time. Based upon the information you obtained from your survey *and* your own personal knowledge of your strengths and weaknesses, choose the attribute of your personality you most need or would like to improve. Then, brainstorm all the possible problems that might arise if that problem were not improved. (Some of these problems you might already have encountered.) For example, if you decided selfishness was the attribute you needed to improve, some possible problems that might arise would be that you might not have many friends; your classmates might not be willing to share resources with you because you do not share with them; or you might not feel very good about yourself when you act selfishly. After you have thought of as many possible problems which relate to the main problem you identified, choose the one are you believe would be best to attack to improve that aspect of your personality. Remember to state your problem as a question beginning with "How might I ...?" or "In what ways might I ...?"

Idea-Finding

Using the question you developed in Problem-Finding, brainstorm as many solutions to your problem as possible. Record *all* of your ideas, no matter how wild they might be. Try to come up with at least 15 ideas.

Solution-Finding

Looking at your list of possible solutions, choose the five that you like best. Now, develop five criteria that will help you choose the best possible solutions. Place your solutions and your criteria on the grid and rank them based on one criterion at a time. Which solution received the most points? This is the solution you will be using in Acceptance-Finding.

Evaluation Grid
Heroic Qualities

Ideas	CR 1	CR 2	CR 3	CR 4	CR 5	TOTAL

Acceptance-Finding

Using your best solution (as determined by Solution-Finding), come up with a plan for putting your solution into action. Think about *who* will be involved in your plan, *when* and *where* your plan will take place, *what* will be involved in your plan, *why* your plan is a good one, and *how* you will put it into action. You might answer the "how" question by listing all the steps in your plan and then putting them in a logical order. Remember to describe your plan in as much detail as possible.

Describe your plan:

_____

_____

_____

_____

_____

_____

_____

_____

_____

_____

_____

_____

_____

_____

_____

_____

_____

_____

_____

Chapter 4
Secondary CPS Activities

Spin-Off

The authors created this creative problem solving simulation while working with a class of junior high school students. The class was part of a collection of mini-courses from which students could choose. The course was designed to give students a number of experiences with various problem solving processes.

Students role-played a government faced with an onslaught of immigrants, and they participated in a simulation that placed them on another planet where they met the troubles colonists to any "new world" might face. Yet, the students didn't seem interested. They seemed more concerned with Mutant Ninja Turtles or the latest teen rock sensation than with the problems on international immigration.

Well, when Mohammed will not come to the mountain ... The authors realized that they would have to provide the students with a new, highly relevant simulation if they were to make creative problem solving seem worthwhile for the group. "Spin-Off"—a creative problem solving mess involving censorship of rock music—was the solution.

While handouts for students to use in small groups or independently have been provided with this activity, *it is suggested that teachers use this simulation as a whole group-activity*. Using broad sheets of butcher paper taped to the classroom walls and large markers, the teacher acts as facilitator, writing student ideas on the butcher paper as they are voiced.

By using the handouts that follow as a guide, a teacher and class new to the creative problem solving process can learn the process together in this whole group fashion. Using this activity with the entire class will allow the teacher to model the process for students before they attack a mess such as that presented in "Tune Town's Troubles" in small groups. Further, it allows the teacher to monitor the degree to which students have developed a proficiency in both divergent and convergent thinking. Of course, if students are already familiar with the creative problem solving process, they may work in small groups using the included handouts.

Spin Off!

Mess-Finding

In this activity, your group will deal with a mess related to the censorship of pop music. Your group will play the parts of music store owners who are faced with many local parent and religious groups that are calling for increased censorship of pop music due to increased violence, sexual content, and mature themes. Lately, the groups have been talking about boycotting your store or picketing outside it to force you to prevent minors from buying what they consider to be obscene music. Your goal in this creative problem solving session is to develop a creative solution for dealing with this mess.

The parent group is vocal. They want you to start labeling records that contain obscene materials and not sell those albums to minors. Some are even calling for you to use a rating system similar to that used for movies. One parent spokesperson explains the need for labeling as she sees it. "Look, I'm not one of those ultra-conservatives who doesn't want children to be exposed to anything more controversial than *Leave It to Beaver*, but I think there ought to be limits. I listened to my thirteen-year-old son's Too Live Crew tape when all of the controversy about them began. The stuff was terrible—graphic descriptions of sex and language that was awful. Worse, in my opinion, was the fact that women in the songs were considered no better than animals. I'm a responsible parent, I want my son to have freedom. I want him to hear ideas that are not necessarily my own, but the kind of trash I heard on that album was just too much.

"Furthermore, I don't understand what is wrong with labeling obscene record albums. I would even be in favor of a rating system like they have for the movies. I have heard some people say that parents ought to be more responsible—that parents, not the record store, ought to be the ones monitoring their children's records and tapes. Well, that kind of thinking might be all right with children younger than ten or eleven, but I can't monitor my thirteen-year-old son's every behavior or record album. He's growing up. I want him to have some freedom. Yet, as a parent I want to have some protections for him as well. I just don't see why some people oppose a labeling program or a rating system for music.

"If that record store doesn't act fast, we just might have to get folks in this community to boycott the store. If all those store owners listen to is money, we might just be able to hit them where it hurts the most—their pocket books."

Individuals and groups in the record industry oppose labels and rating systems. Such systems, they claim, restrict the free sharing of ideas guaranteed in the First Amendment. Furthermore, because such systems effect sales, they say that it, in essence, controls the content of the music they record and sell.

One musician explains his concern over this issue. "I don't think these parents and religious groups have a grasp on this thing. First of all, just because a kid listens to what the parents call objectionable music, that doesn't mean that the kid is going to be corrupted by it or anything. Look at Britain. They have no restriction on who can buy music and they have a lot lower crime rate and drug use rate. When you really ask teenagers, most don't even listen to the words of the songs they hear.

"The worst part of the whole thing is that the labels or rating systems are going to effect sales and that means that the content of the music will be changed. Think about it. Let's say I make a CD with questionable lyrics which would win my CD one of those obscenity labels. Knowing that that label will lower sales, what record company would buy my work? Oh, sure, if I were Mick Jagger or something, they might buy it, but I'm not. The result is that I'll be forced to conform my music to whatever these parent groups call acceptable, and as I remember, the First Amendment protects me from something like that—doesn't it? At any rate, store owners that give in to these groups are just cowards as far as I'm concerned."

To make matters more complicated, local teens have entered the debate. "Look, it doesn't really matter if the local record store labels or rates the music they sell," one teenager explained. "The town of Barksville is just five miles away. If any of us really want to buy a restricted album, we'll just go there. In fact, since we'll probably just go there for the rest of our records and CDs if the local store starts labeling music, the local store is going to loose about 75 percent of its business. The parent groups may be the ones raising the stink, but we are the ones who buy the music—shouldn't our wants come first?"

As the owners of a record store, what solution will you be able to design?

Data-Finding

Who is involved in this mess?

Who might be harmed because of adolescents exposed to violence, sexual content, or mature themes in music?

What are some ways music affects people's behaviors?

What are some of the opinions involved (consider both sides of the issue)?

What has been done in similar situations to address this type of mess?

Where is the support for censorship likely to be most intense in your community?

Where is the opposition for censorship likely to be most intense in your community?

What are some of the social, economic, and moral consequences of violent, sexual, or mature content in music to which adolescents listen?

What are some of the social, economic, and moral consequences of censoring, labeling, or rating the content of music?

What are some of your personal feelings about this issue?

Do you think the teenagers are serious about going to another store to buy records?

Problem-Finding

Design at least five problem or challenge statements below. Remember, problem or challenge statements must begin with one of the invitation "stems":

- In what ways might we ...   (IWWMW)
- How might we ...   (HMW)
- How to ...   (H2)

Also, remember that an action verb must be included in the statement (usually, it immediately follows the stem). For example, your group might define a problem statement such as, "In what ways might we [stem] develop [action verb] a music labeling system acceptable to all involved?"

1.

2.

3.

4.

5.

Use the following questions to choose a problem or challenge statement from your list of five.

- To what extent is the problem or challenge significant (relates to the mess)?
- To what extent does the statement address an underlying problem?
- To what extent does the statement lend itself to creative solutions?
- To what extent is the group interested in working with the statement?

Idea-Finding

Below, list at least ten ideas for addressing your problem. Remember to use divergent thinking: don't judge the ideas of others—simply write ideas down as they are spoken, and let those wild ideas flow! A wild idea can always be tamed.

1.

2.

3.

4.

5.

6.

7.

8.

9.

10.

Using the technique of "hits and hot spots," return to your list of ideas and narrow it to five strong ideas. Remember, you may combine two *related* ideas during hits and hot spots.

Solution-Finding

Brainstorm five criteria for evaluating your idea statements. Each criterion should relate to a single aspect of the solution. You may wish to consider such aspects of the solution as time, costs, workability, acceptability, and usefulness. For example, one criterion might be "To what extent will the parent groups, local teenagers, and local musicians find the solution acceptable?"

Criterion 1: To what extent ...

Criterion 2: To what extent ...

Criterion 3: To what extent ...

Criterion 4: To what extent ...

Criterion 5: To what extent ...

Evaluate your ideas using the evaluation grid below.

Evaluation Grid						
Ideas	CR 1	CR 2	CR 3	CR 4	CR 5	TOTAL

Acceptance-Finding

Describe those people, things, organizations, events, etc., that you feel will act as assisters or resisters to putting your plan of action in place.

Assisters   **Resisters**

Design a five-step plan for implementing your solution. Your plan should use the assisters you identified above, and it should describe ways to overcome the resisters you identified.

1.

2.

3.

4.

5.

Describe briefly below how you plan to evaluate your action plan. That is, how will you determine that your plan is working?

_____

_____

_____

_____

_____

_____

_____

_____

_____

_____

_____

_____

_____

_____

_____

_____

_____

_____

_____

_____

_____

_____

Tune Town's Troubles

Keep in mind that it is not always necessary to go through every one of the steps in the creative problem solving process. For example, in the following activity, students move into the creative problem solving process at the problem-finding step. This is because the mess is presented to the students in the form of a newspaper article from the *Tune Town Gazette*. The students then gather data about the mess by participating in a simulated town council meeting. Only after the town meeting do students begin formally addressing the issues using the creative problem solving process.

Obviously, this activity is structured quite differently from some of the earlier ones. This difference points to the strength of the creative problem solving process—its flexibility. As you become increasingly familiar with the process, the idea of mixing simulations, role-playing, socio-drama, lectures, and independent research with the various steps of the creative problem solving process will seem quite natural.

Introduce the mess to the students by passing out a copy of the article from the *Tune Town Gazette* (page 109). Ask one student to read the article aloud to the rest of the class. Afterward, explain to the students that the first part of this activity involves their participation in the simulation of the city council meeting discussed in the article.

Next, pass out a copy of *Roles—Tune Town's Troubles* and the *Role/Reason Creation* sheets to each student. Pick or allow students to choose those who will play the city council members. Divide the rest of the students evenly between the "Against the Curfew" and the "For the Curfew" *Role/Reason Creation* Sheets.

While the rest of the class fills out the sheets, instruct the council members to generate some questions that they feel they either need or want to know about the public's perception of the issue with which they will deal.

When everyone is ready, the simulation may begin. The students may adhere to either the *City Council Meeting Procedures* sheet or some other set of guidelines that the teacher wishes followed. When the chairperson draws the meeting to a close, the students should move into small working groups for the closed-door, working session.

While every student should be provided with all the closed-door, working session handouts, the teacher may want to ask that only one set of handouts be filled out by each group. Once the students begin work, the teacher may move from group to group helping groups that reach snags or otherwise experience trouble.

This lesson could easily be extended by allowing students to deal with a real issue faced by their own city council or school board. It would be quite valuable to have the students spend an evening at a city council or school board meeting and observe the events and information discussed. The information learned from such a field-trip could then act as the data-finding step for a new problem that the class could address.

Tune Town's Troubles

Mess-Finding and Data-Finding

Excerpted from the <u>Tune Town Gazette</u>, Sunday, October 27, 1991.

Richardson Heights Residents to Petition for Curfew

Residents of the Richardson Heights district of Tune Town will go before the city council Monday night in hopes of persuading the council to pass restrictions on use of the city's outdoor theater after 10:30 p.m. The residents claim that noise from late night music concerts such as the recent Black Lizard concert is so loud as to keep residents up into the early hours of the morning.

John Waterman, a long-time Heights resident explained the group's position. "It is not that we don't like music. It's just that we're losing sleep because of these concerts. I'm a foreman at the local plastics plant, and I've got to get up at five in the morning in order to get to work for the morning shift. But these concerts often last until 12:30 a.m. Often, I drag around all day because I've only gotten four hours of sleep."

Jo Ann Petters, another Richardson Heights resident, explained, "If the concerts were not so loud that would be one thing, but it's not at all unusual for me to lie in bed at night and hear a whole concert as if a radio were playing right in the room with me. Some nights, my bed even vibrates with the beats of the base drums.

"This just isn't fair. My husband and I bought our house in Richardson Heights district of Tune Town in order to get away from the noise and bustle of some of the other districts of the city. It just isn't fair."

Others are not so sure. Mark Whitman, who is responsible for booking many of the concerts at the outdoor theater, explained that the theater was built in 1971—years before most Richardson Heights residents had bought their homes. "They knew about the outdoor theater when they bought their homes. In fact, the noise levels resulting from the concerts is one of the reasons homes in the Richardson Heights area are less expensive than in other similar areas of town. The homes in Richardson Heights sell for as much as 10% less than those in the lake area—an area of homes very similar to those in Richardson Heights. When they bought their homes they got a cheaper deal because of the concerts, and now they don't want to put up with the noise of the concerts. They want it both ways."

R. Perry, the chairperson of the council, had little to say about the controversy other than that the council would hear both sides of the discussion at the Monday city council meeting. Perry did say that the council members plan to keep an open mind about the issue.

The council is expected to hear from both sides of the issue Monday night at its 7:00 p.m. meeting.

Roles—Tune Town's Troubles

The City Council Members

R. Perry: As the chair of the city council, it is your responsibility to see that the meeting runs smoothly and that all wishing to share their views are heard. At this point, no one knows how you feel about the curfew. You feel your decision can be made only after hearing from both sides.

B. Johnson: Your home is in the Richardson Heights section of Tune Town. In fact, this issue has been the topic of much concern at many of the parties you have attended of late. You would like to see the issue resolved quickly.

J. Hamilton: You are not sure the outdoor theater is such a good idea anyway. The maintenance on the building and clean-up crew necessary to keep the theater open simply don't seem worth the effort. The small net profit of $50,000 the theater brings in for the city seems little compensation for the controversy it causes. But, it seems to you that restrictions on concert times might even reduce the theater's profits all the more.

R. Thomas: You have two teenagers who enjoy going to concerts at the outdoor theater. It seems to you to be a safe environment for young people to gather and enjoy themselves on a weekend night. You would hate to see the outdoor theater closed, but you don't see why a reasonable curfew might not be imposed.

P. Perkins: You have been concerned for a long time that the outdoor theater was becoming a hang-out for "thugs." It was originally built to bring cultural experiences to the people of Tune Town, but, now, it has become little more than a concert hall for rock-and-roll bands and country-and-western bands, and a gathering place for a "bad element."

L. Lake: A concert fan yourself, you would hate to see restrictions on the outdoor theater. One of your favorite pastimes on a weekend night is to take your spouse to dinner and then go to the outdoor theater for live entertainment. "Certainly better than a night of T.V.," you have often commented.

Other Roles: The other roles in this simulation are created by the students participating in the simulation. Using the *Role/Reasons Creation Form*, students will design their own character and that character's beliefs concerning the curfew idea.

Role/Reason Creation Form

Position: AGAINST a Curfew

Instructions: In the following activity, you will create a character and the reasons that character believes as he or she does concerning the curfew for the outdoor theater.

Your Name:

Name of Character:

Physical Features:

Hair Color: Height: Age:

Noticeable or Unique Features:

Family Status (single, married, children):

Section of Town in Which You Live (Circle One):

Richardson Heights   Lake Hills   East Side
   (middle income)   (upper-middle income)   (lower income)

List Five Possible Reasons why your character opposes the curfew (consider the effect such an action might have on any concert theater and consider the benefits late-night concerts might offer):

Circle the Reason that you believe will influence the city council's decision the most, or target a single council member, and circle the single reason that might influence that council member the most.

Elaborate on the Circled Reason by thinking of at least two specific details that would support that reason. For example, if you say that the curfew will reduce the theater's profits, think of at least two ways that the profits would be reduced.

Role/Reason Creation Form

Position: FOR a Curfew

Instructions: In the following activity, you will create a character and the reasons that character believes as he or she does concerning the curfew for the outdoor theater.

Your Name:

Name of Character:

Physical Features:

Hair Color: Height: Age:

Noticeable or Unique Features:

Family Status (single, married, children):

Section of Town in Which You Live (Circle One):

Richardson Heights   Lake Hills   East Side
   (middle income)   (upper-middle income)   (lower income)

List Five Possible Reasons why your character is for the curfew (consider the effect such an action might have on any concert theater and consider the benefits a curfew might offer the parties involved):

Circle the Reason that you believe will influence the city council's decision the most, or target a single council member, and circle the single reason that might influence that council member the most.

Elaborate on the Circled Reason by thinking of at least two specific details that would support that reason. For example, if you say that the curfew will improve property values in the area, give two ways that such an increase might be desirable for a city and its government.

City Council Meeting Procedures

1. Before the meeting begins, a speakers list should be passed around the room. Each character should be listed on the speakers list. The council's chairperson will call on speakers to address the council in the order that they signed the speakers list.

2. The chairperson, R. Perry, will call the meeting to order. The chair will then ask all to rise and say the Pledge of Allegiance.

3. Then R. Perry will say the following:

    Ladies and gentlemen, the issue that I believe most of you have gathered to address tonight is that of the outdoor theater. As your city council, we want to address this issue in the most fair and reasonable fashion possible. To do that, it is necessary for the council to gather data related to the issue from both sides. This week's meeting is only to hear ideas—for the council to become more aware of the issues involved. Specific solutions to the issue will be developed by the council soon after this meeting in a special session.

    We do, however, ask that for the sake of time, all speeches related to this issue be no longer than 60 seconds. Furthermore, speakers should understand that at the conclusion of a speech the council members may wish to pose some questions to the speaker, but these question and answer sessions will be limited to 60 seconds.

    Now, let us begin ...

4. The chair will now refer to the speakers list and ask the first speaker to come before the council. When speaker one has spoken and the council has had a chance to ask any questions they deem necessary, the next speaker will be called and so on.

5. After each person on the speakers list has spoken, the chair will thank the speakers for sharing their information and explain that the council will now move into a closed-door, working session wherein it will resolve the issue of the outdoor theater. The chair will then conclude the meeting.

Closed-Door, Working Session

Problem-Finding

Instructions: In this phase of the activity, you will work in a group using four steps of the six-step Creative Problem Solving process to accomplish the following:

- to identify a single problem associated with the issue of the outdoor theater
- to identify a solution for the problem
- to create a plan of action that will successfully carry out your solution

Because you must be able to use your full creative and critical talents to address this issue, you should no longer be playing a role from the simulation. Just be yourself and work to generate the best possible solution for this issue. First, based upon your own ideas and opinions and the information you heard in the city council meeting, work as a group to identify at least ten possible problem statements related to the issue of the outdoor theater. Of course, you may generate many more than ten but generate at least that many. Remember, all should begin with one of the following stems: "In what ways might we ...?" or "How might we ...?"

1.

2.

3.

4.

5.

6.

7.

8.

9.

10.

Closed-Door, Working Session

Problem-Finding (Cont.)

Once you have identified the ten, circle the ideas that individuals in your group consider to be "hits" (i.e., problems that seem especially important). Keep in mind that if any one person believes an idea to be a hit, then it is one and it should be circled.

Next, look over the ideas you have circled. Do some of your ideas relate in such a way that you could group them? Is it possible to write problem statements that are broad enough to include those statements that you could group together? If so, add those statements to your list. These broader problem statements are called "hot spots."

Finally, pick the problem statement from your hits and hot spots that you feel (1) a city council would have the greatest influence over, (2) would require a creative solution, and (3) seems most critical or important.

Write your single, chosen problem statement in the blank below.

_____

_____

_____

_____

_____

_____

Closed-Door, Working Session

Idea-Finding

Brainstorm as many ideas as you can that would address your problem statement. Remember the rules of brainstorming ...

- Don't judge ideas generated until after the brainstorming session
- Wild ideas are encouraged
- Work to generate lots of ideas
- Try to combine or build off of the ideas of others

_____

_____

_____

_____

_____

_____

_____

_____

_____

_____

_____

_____

_____

_____

_____

When your group is finished brainstorming, use the technique of hits and hot spots discussed in the problem-finding step to narrow your list of ideas down to just those your groups feels are the hits and hot spots. In the next step, you will narrow your list even further.

Closed-Door, Working Session

Solution-Finding

Now, use the rules of brainstorming to help your group brainstorm a number of possible criteria you might use to evaluate your solutions. For example, if you feel that cost is a concern, one criterion might be "To what extent will this solution be inexpensive?" Try to generate as many criteria to evaluate your solutions as possible.

_____

_____

_____

_____

_____

_____

_____

_____

_____

_____

_____

_____

_____

_____

_____

_____

_____

_____

Now, as a group, choose the five criteria your group feels to be most important. Remember, it is with these criteria that you will choose your best solution, so make sure everyone can agree on which criteria is best. Consider both the criteria that you feel a good solution *must* meet and the criteria you *want* your solution to meet.

Closed-Door, Working Session

Solution-Finding

It is now time to select the strongest solution for your problem statement. Use the evaluation grid below to select a solution. It is always a good idea to check that the ideas you plan to include on the evaluation grid will meet your *musts* criteria. If an idea does not meet this minimum standard, modify it so that it does. Also, remember that it is always possible to modify a solution so that it will receive a higher score. For instance, if you feel a good solution is too expensive and might receive a lower score on a criterion related to expense, try to modify the solution so that it will be cheaper to implement.

Evaluation Grid						
Ideas	CR 1	CR 2	CR 3	CR 4	CR 5	TOTAL

Closed-Door, Working Session

Acceptance-Finding

In this, the last step of the creative problem solving process, you will identify the various people and resources that might assist you as you try to put your solution into action. Then you will identify those people and resources that might resist your efforts.

Once the assisters and resisters to your solution have been identified, you should write a paragraph or essay that describes the actions that will have to be taken to put your solution into effect. The paragraph or essay ought to explain how you might put your assisters to use and how you might overcome the resisters to your plan. This paragraph or essay will be read to the rest of the class.

Assisters:

Resisters:

Plan of Action:
The group should agree on a specific plan of action before the paragraph or essay is written. Write the steps in your plan below.

1.

2.

3.

4.

5.

References

Caroll, B. (1990). A hard look into the future. *The Prufrock Journal*, 1 (3): 15-17.

Dacey, J (1989). *Fundamentals of creative thinking*. Lexington: Lexington Books.

Dacey, J & Ripple, R. (1967). The facilitation of problem solving and verbal creativity by exposure to programmed instruction. *Psychology in the schools*, 4 (3), 240-245.

Eberle, R. (1971). *Scamper: games for imagination development*. Buffalo: D.O.K.

Isaksen, S. and Treffinger, D. (1985). *Creative problem solving: the basic course*. Buffalo: Bearly Limited.

Osborn, A. (1963). *Applied imagination*. New York: Charles Scribners Sons.

Parnes, S. (1985). *A facilitating style of leadership*. Buffalo, New York: Bearly Limited.

Parnes, S., Noller, R., and Biondi, A. (1976). *Creative action book*. New York: Charles Scribners Sons.

Parnes, S., Noller, R., and Biondi, A. (1977). *Guide to creative action*. New York: Charles Scribners Sons.

Torrance, E. (1979). *The search for satori & creativity*. Buffalo: Bearly Limited.

Torrance, E. (1979). *Education and the creative potential*. Minneapolis: University of Minnesota Press.

Torrance, E. (1962). *Guiding creative talent*. Englewood Cliffs: Prentice-Hall.

Treffinger, D. and Sortore, M. (1990). Creative problem solving — the need, the process, the metamorphosis. *The Prufrock Journal*, 2 (2), 6-15.

Treffinger, D., Isaksen, S., and Firestien, R. (1982). *Handbook of creative learning*. New York: Center for Creative Learning.